Smma

A Complete Guide How to Start
Social Media Marketing Agency
With Zero Capital

*(How to Start Your Own Social Media Marketing
Agency)*

Wilma Halbert

Published By **Jordan Levy**

Wilma Halbert

Smma: A Complete Guide How to Start Social Media Marketing Agency With Zero Capital (How to Start Your Own Social Media Marketing Agency)

ISBN 978-1-7780579-8-4

Legal & Disclaimer

TABLE OF CONTENTS

Introduction

When it comes to establishing an enterprise there are numerous things you'll need to complete. One of them is establishing your agency. It's the perfect time to start thinking about the kind of niche your agency should be located in. Niche vs general agency.

One of the most important decisions is whether your company should be operating located in a niche market. There are benefits and drawbacks for both. It is possible to specialize in a particular field instead of trying to serve every client who has visited your business.

The advantages to all involved parties are greater regularity, less time spent on clients who may not be working out, and more content employees since they're working on something they like and are skilled at. That's not to suggest that you shouldn't be able to accomplish both of these things, however certain businesses can be "full service" companies that operate across all areas and such companies might have difficulty communicating with clients who are accustomed to a specific marketing firm.

An example would be an all-encompassing agency like The Marketing Group. They're a full-service marketing agency that boasts a impressive client roster which includes Disney and The U.S. Air Force, and a number of important Hollywood studios. They also have a specialization in four areas: tourism, travel food and beverage and real property development. Their specific market knowledge that has enabled their growth to be so rapid in these four specific market segments.

Each market is a bit different, and sometimes controversial events which a business owner might be keen to discuss. If you're not already familiar with the various industries it might be difficult to know what's happening and why these are so important. In this scenario your marketing strategies could be ineffective, or could even harm the reputation of your company.

Your business and your entire business will become more attractive if it is based on an area of focus. There are plenty of things you need to be aware of before beginning searching for your ideal sector, including the latest trends in the market and conditions. However, once you've figured them out the entire process is much more straightforward. The use of niches makes a lot of sense for questions you're afraid to ask because they could be a great way to help a company become more effective.

Chapter 1: Pricing Your Services

Finding a niche market likely to be a lot easier since you'll be dealing with fewer factors. Niches typically have fixed prices, while general marketing campaigns typically vary from client to customer according to the results and the ability to control expectations.

Pricing explained

The service is evaluated in detail , taking the time to comprehend all client requirements and then present them in a professional manner. The valuable information is communicated to the client about what we'll explain in depth in an organized report that is available to those needing support from our team. A pricing model is created by conducting research into the market, service level requirements of clients and other similar aspects.

For example, the marketing on social media is priced according to the amount of followers we'll be able to attract through different social networks like Facebook, Twitter, and others. The price charged is the lowest fixed price system in which there is no room for negotiation.

The models for revenue generated by services are classified into three primary models i.e. cost-plus pricing, value-based and fixed price based upon the level of complexity of services offered. In the cost-plus model, the revenue from services is determined based on the costs of providing a specific product or service and then a profit margin that is added to the cost. In the majority of cases the approach is utilized to price products and services when there is no industry standards that companies can base their price.

The value-based pricing model service revenue is calculated on the basis of the value that is perceived by the client of the service or product and in certain cases, also include nonmonetary elements like effort, time potential risks, other factors. This is another controversial type of pricing model employed by corporations as it assesses the value of their products or services according to the opinion of the customer. In this model, customers are asked to consider their impression of a product or service, in order to decide the amount they're willing to spend for it. A trustworthy courier will charge more for customers who need urgent deliveries but at the same time charging less to those who do not require the product or service in a hurry and could be provided with a specific time during which the goods will be shipped.

The concept of differentiation in service is the ultimate pricing model to be considered by firms when providing consultation services. This can be achieved by distinguishing the services offered by the quality, features or distinctiveness and more. Differentiation can be by combining different factors like the technology used, the time required to implement as well as the methods of managing clients and more.

What can be done?

There are two steps an organization should consider when it decides to take an approach that is unique to its services or products

1.) A shift in the company's operations of general marketing targeted marketing.

2.) The decision on the best service for clients is in light of the market trend.

In the new shift of general marketing targeted marketing, businesses can run targeted ads in accordance with their market. This means that a business will not just advertise its products or services, but also inform clients about what it offers and how it can help them. Every successful business understands the importance of its customer base, as well as the demand for its services or products. Being niche is about altering the way that a business operates, but it can be accomplished without losing potential customers if done correctly.

Charges per hour

The length of time a company is able to offer its product or service for a certain cost is known as project duration. This depends on several variables, such as the type of service offered and the time for development or the time frame for delivery and client expectations.

The fixed-price model in which social media followers are priced will be charging our customers according to the amount of followers that are generated which means we'd be charging customers on a basis of per-follower. There are many online companies who charge higher prices for this type of service. Some companies offer as high as the price of $ 10 per 100 followers, but we at Social Media Marketing Business we insist on a low-cost structure while still providing top-quality products and services to our customers.

In terms of the length of the project is concerned, there's no set duration, however it is a clearly defined minimum requirement to us here in Social Media Marketing Business and it is all hours.

In terms of followers on social media are concerned, we'd provide followers from different platforms, including Facebook, Twitter, Instagram and more. We want to advertise the businesses of our clients to their market of choice efficiently that is possible. This is the reason the reason why Social Media Marketing Business Social Media Marketing Business offer social media followers that are focused on specific segments of the population. Being a niche player in the field of social media marketing can't be achieved without separating your company from the rest and that is exactly our primary concentrate on.

If you have the right approach, by using Facebook and Twitter ads , you can advertise your products or services to thousands of highly targeted customers around the world.

Since social media marketing began to gain traction it has become essential for businesses to offer their customers with products and services related to this industry as it is one of the most significant market on the internet currently. Because an enormous number of people utilize social media daily it is easy for businesses to establish a presence on the platform and grow their client base. It is a two-way communications platform that allows businesses to connect directly with their prospective customers and build powerful relationships that can will lead to more business transactions.

Social Media Marketing Business is a full-service digital marketing company located within Santa Clara, California. Our offerings comprise Web Design & Development, SEO Service, SMO

Service, PPC Service, E-mail Marketing as well as Social Media Services. We strive to create innovative strategies and solutions targeted at the customers to maximize the benefit of market opportunities that are emerging.

Affiliate Marketing is regarded as a form of revenue sharing scheme where the owners receive a payment when clients purchase or book a flight on the internet. It falls under the umbrella of online marketing and is growing in recognition among small companies bloggers, bloggers, and affiliate marketers.

The process of launching an affiliate site by yourself can be an extremely difficult task if you do not have experience in this particular field, or more difficult if you don't know what to do with code. The team of Social Media Marketing Business Social Media Marketing Business will help you design a professional-looking website that is able to draw in targeted visitors, which is the primary aim.

In terms of affiliate marketing, you must include an affiliate programme that is suitable for every business model available as well as an affiliate network that includes a variety of well-known products, in order to be promoted by the affiliate program...

Every business must have a robust presence on social media to build greater awareness of the business and increase sales for customers. Facebook ads provide businesses with an online platform on which they can communicate with potential customers with no extra cost; just make a post and make sure to target the right target audience.

Pinterest is among the top platforms you can utilize to connect with a huge amount of people, even if they're not actively searching for brands or products similar to yours within their own local areas. The concept for Pinterest marketing is straightforward, users search and pin pictures on this platform to save them to use later.

If you are looking to draw new customers to your business it is recommended to provide them with a free ebook which will assist them in one way or other way. This is particularly important for businesses who are just trying to establish themselves on the internet; they require to get as much positive feedback as possible from various independent sources.

But, charging by the hour can mean that there's an enormous gap between what the contractor defines as the absolute minimum they can charge and what you consider your own most basic requirements to be. It could be that you feel they're working too slow or inefficiently, however, charging per hour implies that there is no means to accelerate them without increasing the price. This could cause a lot of conflict later on when it comes to billing.

A fixed-fee agreement is an option that is becoming more popular because it reduces the chance of overcharging your project the hourly cost. It also makes sure that you aren't paid for clock time that the contractor isn't even working in any way, which could occur if they bill per hour.

Project that is based

The location where the project is located is crucial since you'll need to work with employees of the specific country. It does not matter if they're in a different timezone than you, however it will matter in the event that they don't have English as their first language and you don't have the local dialect.

As we've said before communication is crucial when working with a partner. If they're not able to communicate in a manner that you can understand, the work will be delayed or completed poorly or in a way that isn't very good.

Your lawyer must be aware of the different laws that apply to people who work and live abroad If any concerns raise concerns, they must be able to provide advice regarding how they might impact your project.

If, for instance, you have a freelancer who dies in death, their estate could have a claim to unpaid fees against the contract agreement they agreed to prior to their demise; such a claim can only be applicable in the country where the contract was concluded. The agreement won't apply in the country where the deceased was domiciled and you must determine which jurisdiction has the final say in the who who.

This type of contract is likely to be ideal for medium or large-scale projects that are likely take time to finish. If you're looking to work on a freelancer who is a solo or smaller team, it might be a trouble to develop the entire plan for your project in one go.

You might not know what you're looking to find with regards to design, or in terms of technology to use until you've looked at some examples of different candidates, and the fixed-price contract may become too rigid as you progress with it.

Instead of making you commit to a lengthy project that cannot be altered or completed in the way you'd like Retainer contracts be a way of paying for the services that are performed.

Retainer agreements are great in situations where you wish to modify the product or service you offer over time or are more flexible with modifications to the scope of your business, and you can also hire freelancing workers to cover the gaps without getting too costly.

If your business is only getting started, then you might not be able afford the cost of a contract such as this from the beginning. If, however, you're working with a reputable agency who has been executing marketing via social media for businesses for at the least a year, they'll be able to offer you an exact proposal for services that cost less the same amount.

Value determined by

It is crucial to consider value in the creation of an effective agency. If you're planning to start an agency just simply for the sake of it and not to make a difference, it's going be difficult for you. You must have some reason to be able to justify for people to select your company over the ones they're currently using.

The idea of establishing an agency on value is the correct decision to make. That is you should base your organization on the value it could provide to individuals. When you decide to create or start an agency, you must be thinking about the value you are offering to the individuals. Value is crucial when you are creating the brand. Your brand's image will be built on the value your business can provide.

Marketing via social media has become extremely popular in recent times that you must ensure that your company is skilled in this area. Specialization in marketing can aid an agency in making more sales, as a large number of brands won't be identified if it is an overall agency. This is due to the fact that there would be competition between all agencies, which could possibly result in one needing to shut down. Niche marketing can help establish a solid image for your company since you can promote your services you are offering to people more effectively.

The creation of an agency around social media marketing is going to mean that you will have many people who are likely to partner with you. This is because this area of marketing is extremely crucial nowadays, and a lot of companies are focused on it, regardless of whether they're big or small. When you set up an agency that is based around social media, you'll be able to hire good people much easier, as there are plenty of applicants for these positions and this will provide you with an advantage.

It is crucial to ensure that your business will to succeed on the market. There are many kinds of brands, which means you have to create something distinctive for your business to be different. It is possible to accomplish this because it allows you to make your brand stand out from the crowd.

The process of creating an agency isn't simple, but it can be rewarding if make it happen. There are many companies that offer the management of social media for businesses today. This means you'll need come up with something distinctive in order to succeed. Making something unique isn't simple however, when you master it, you're likely be able to earn lots of money.

An effective agency is about the way you treat clients and the value you can offer them. If you'd like your business to be successful on the market, this must be always on the forefront of your agenda. This is because providing quality services must be at the top of your list of priorities if you wish to gain the trust of customers.

To ensure that your company will succeed, the most effective thing to do is market your company effectively. This will allow you to attract lots of clients and that can translate into profit. If you do not market your company effectively, it's difficult to attract clients. This can result in lots of problems.

The creation of a strong branding strategy is essential for being successful in the marketplace. When you are branding your business, you have to think of something that is unique however, there are many firms out there and coming up with something unique may be challenging.

Create your business plan

A business plan can be much more than just an strategy of your own business. A thorough and well-thought out planning for your business can be the ideal method of getting others to join. It's the first step to receiving investors, obtaining an loan from a bank or even funding your venture with your savings.

Planning is a crucial element of any business venture. It helps you establish goals and goals that you will later be able follow when you begin your company. It takes time , but it can be extremely rewarding after it has been completed.

The necessity to create the business plan is essential if you plan to seek assistance from outside. Even if you're not planning on launching the investment rounds or taking an loan, your company requires the right direction. A solid business plan can provide that direction and to establish the base that you require to start your business.

Chapter 2: Write An Business Plan

Business plans are basically lengthy documents that outline the purpose of your business and the way you intend to accomplish it. It outlines the items or services you intend to offer, what they'll cost, the intended market, as well as the method by which you'll be successful.

An investor or loan officer would like to study the business plan before looking at your figures. If you're unable to clearly explain the purpose of your business and why it's a success and the way you intend to improve your chances of success for yourself in the near future the chances are nobody else is likely to be either.

Here's a brief overview of the sections you should include within your plan of business:

*Business Overview It is a brief introduction to your business and the things you do. It must be able to be a stand-alone document and be able to make sense to investors and others who aren't familiar with how your company operates.

The overview of the brand or company is a concise summary of the company's history and achievements, as well as any noteworthy accomplishments, and advantages over competitors. The aim for this part is to describe how your business is different than your competitors and the way you intend to make the most of your strengths.

*Market overview - List your customers by their demographics and psychographics. Define how the company plans to reach its intended market. Define the traits of prospective customers, their requirements as well as their wants and purchasing patterns. Examine any competition currently within the industry or market where your business may have to compete and differentiate its position.

*Product/service overview: Describe the service or product that your business sells, as well as the benefits and features. Explain the unique features of your product and how they will benefit customers. Define the intended market for the service or product and the method of distribution and how licensing arrangements are to be concluded.

Forecast of revenue and sales Based on market research, figure out the amount you'll sell during the first year of operation as well as every year thereafter. Include estimates of sales for each major service or product line by market or territory segment, or at retail and wholesale prices. Include any other ancillary sources of business , such as services or sales to other businesses and individuals, franchising fees or licensing revenue.

*Competitive analysis: Describe the competitive elements in your industry and then consider ways to differentiate yourself from your competition. Consider what other businesses have accomplished to be successful in this area and the way you intend on making it better.

*Marketing/sales strategy Outline your sales and marketing strategies, which include the use of referrals from customers loyalty programs and repeat customers and referred business from other businesses, and personal selling efforts of employees of management. Include a review of possible markets for your major products or services. Consider how you will monitor progress towards your the goals.

*Distribution strategy - List the distribution routes you plan to use to reach customers, including the kind of delivery vehicles as well as other support services for sales. Discuss any agreements you intend to make with manufacturers wholesalers, distributors, etc. advertise your product, etc.

What are the reasons you need a business Plan

The business planning process is among the foundations about the success of a business. The right business plan will allow your business grow and eliminate the uncertainty about how to go about your business effectively. It will also provide individuals who would like to finance or invest in your business with an understanding of what you're looking to achieve and how you plan to achieve it, and whether or not they are interested in participating in your venture.

Most financial institutions, like banks will require you to submit a plan prior to seeking loans or financing. A thorough and well-written business plan will definitely assist you in obtaining the funding you require to see your company increase in size.

When it comes to the establishment of a business, it is essential for the business owner (the person who came up with the concept and is managing the company) to create a clear and precise business plan that outlines how they will implement their business ideas into existence. It must also detail what the future prospects of the business will be after it has introduced the product on the market, and other.

Students should think about making a business plan if they are looking to learn about the details in business management. This process can give them an understanding about how companies are constructed and run as well as how they are maintained.

A business plan may be used as a emergency guide to consult whenever you're stuck or aren't sure how to proceed. It can help you identify the strengths and weaknesses of your business , which could be utilized to improve in the future.

If you intend to sell or transfer your business to others it's an ideal idea to draft an official business plan that will serve as a reference to the new owner about how to manage and maintain the business.

A business plan is an instrument you can utilize in setting your goals and goals. When it is completed, it will aid you in determining the gaps in between the current situation and where you'd like your company will be by the near future to allow you to begin thinking about ways to bridge the gap.

The goal of the above is not just to create an outline of your business plan to assist you in getting loans from banks or various financial institutions. It is rather to be armed with the right information about your business that can act as a reference when you are stuck. In this regard it is suggested that you spend time writing down the specifics of how you are planning to do in your company and the way you plan to achieve it.

The process of writing a business plan not need to be difficult. Follow these steps and ensure that you record all the details of your company in full detail:

1.Determine the type of business you would like to create - it can be a new venture or an existing one. the most important aspect here is that you are aware of the kind of business you wish to manage. A few of the kinds of companies you can pick from include a service-based franchise-based business, a product-based one and eCommerce. It's up to you , but make sure it helps you achieve your goals and objectives.

2.Create your rough draft and note down any concepts you've come up with about what you would like your business to develop. Write down every detail as well as the details of what you need to do to make your business successful. This includes details like the products or services you offer clients, the target market, the management team, the where you will locate your office or manufacturing facility and much more. Note everything you would like your business to become in the future . This will be your reference as you work on it.

3.Make an organized plan of each step Once you have a outline of what you want to accomplish with your business, you should create an outline of your work schedule to help you get to your target. Your plan should be as specific as possible , and stay clear of broad declarations or vague concepts that you may overlook later. Make sure to write everything in full detail to ensure that no one is able to misunderstand what you're trying to achieve.

4.Put everything in the correct form - making it look attractive by arranging them in accordance with their function and then placing them in charts and graphs whenever feasible.

5.Hire an expert to help in the final draft of your plan It is not unusual when business proposals get criticized or rejected by lenders for lack of an appropriate presentation. This includes formatting and grammar, organization of content, and spelling mistakes, in addition to other things. This can result in your plan being viewed as unprofessional and not being taken seriously. It is also possible that you require assistance from a professional if you have no experience or background in the writing of business plans.

6.Approach potential lenders. Once your business plan is approved by the lending institution, the plan could be used for a loan so you can begin to implement what you've planned. It is possible that you will need to modify the plan in line with the information you received through your loan provider.

Business Description

A business's description plays a crucial function in letting people be aware of the benefits that the business provides and what it provides to the marketplace. The description should be clearly written to convey the message. This is an excellent chance to explain what you're offering them and the reasons why they should partner with you. Keep in mind that the goal for this page is to provide potential customers a glimpse of your company's offerings and what it can do for them.

Two sentences in the first paragraph should draw the attention of potential buyers. A convincing description can attract buyers who will continue reading and scrutinize the completeness of your information. If the initial two sentences don't succeed, the following will be not read.

It is recommended to keep the text short, around 100-150 words since this area is searched on several places, including Google or Bing and users don't have the time to go through a lot of text. In this section, you must discuss Digital Marketing Agency | Social Media Marketing Business.

The description of your business should be interesting and include the advantages of your company. There is a great chance to attract more leads than competitors since the description serves as an opportunity to present yourself that you are an professional in the field of Digital Marketing Agency | Social Media Marketing Business and also what distinguishes you from other. Your aim is to generate more leads, and you must discuss Digital Marketing Agency | Social Media Marketing Business in an approach that is able to reach prospective buyers.

Information about Us

Now , your readers are wondering what makes them pick you over the other options? It's crucial to provide the answer and explain your readers why you're the best and distinct from other businesses offering the same services. It is essential to always be able to demonstrate an USP (Unique Selling Proposition). This section plays a significant part in establishing confidence and trust.

It is recommended to keep photographs of your workplace and team members, prizes, and accomplishments. You should be extremely cautious regarding the quality of images that you upload. If they're not up to par then you'll be unable to gain the trust of your prospective customers.

This is where you can discuss Digital Marketing Agency | Social Media Marketing Business. Provide a concise description of the person you are, the services you provide and the reasons why they need to collaborate with you. Your business might have recently been established or has been in operation for a long time; it is vital to mention the duration of your business in this section since it helps build confidence. Potential customers might be skeptical of the longevity of your company, therefore you need to convince them that you're the right choice for them.

Services We Offer

This is the most crucial section of any site as it describes your company's services and the services it offers. Prospective buyers conduct a basic search through Google as well as Bing to find out more about your offerings. It's crucial to list every service you offer since it will help clients make their decision quickly and easily. Note down what sets you apart from your competitors. Digital Marketing Agency | Social Media Marketing Companies or your competitors.

The content of this section can differ for companies based on their structure, so it's up to you to decide on the content for this part. However, it is crucial to mention your offerings and offer specific advantages. The most well-known services are SEO, PPC, Social Media Optimization, Web Designing, graphic designing and more.

You are always welcome to add the URL to your portfolio so viewers can look over the work you've accomplished for others in Digital Marketing Agency | Social Media Marketing Business.

It is important to discuss Digital Marketing Agency | Social Media Marketing Business which includes SEO, PPC, Social Media Optimization and more. You must conduct research into the needs of your customers and demonstrate how you can satisfy the needs of your customers with your services. Start by listing your entire range of services you offer and then break down each one into detail.

Be specific and discuss Digital Marketing Agency | Social Media Marketing Business in way that your readers are able to comprehend your offerings. If you're not equipped with enough knowledge or resources, you can admit that. It's always better apologize than to trick potential customers into believing that you have false information.

People love to watch pictures. It's always a good idea to include photos of your website staff members, team members, as well as your office.

It is important to let your customers understand why they should work with you on Digital Marketing Agency | Social Media Marketing Business? What are the motives that drive them to do it? You must describe the various services you offer and why they are different from the rest. This is crucial as it allows prospective clients know what you can offer them.

If you're an independent contractor, this is the most crucial since it explains the Digital Marketing Agency | Social Media Marketing Business specifically you'll do for them. You must create a thorough outline of how long it will take to complete and when you can expect to see outcomes.

If you're a firm or an agency, this section is not required to include. It is easy to jump directly between "Our Services" to the pricing and packages section.

If it's a large budget, then describe the Digital Marketing Agency | Social Media Marketing Business in full to let visitors know what they can expect from their budget. If It's a budget-friendly project, it's not essential to include this section. In certain cases you can jump straight from "We provide" into the packages and pricing section.

If you're running an Digital Marketing Agency | Social Media Marketing Business or other type of business it is essential to give complete information about the team members. Customers are interested in knowing who is working on their project. It is better to include the photos that your members of the team, so that they learn more about your team. They can also connect directly with them through phone calls, email or other means.

Beware of scams by including an adequately written disclaimer to this section. Scams are a common occurrence among Digital Marketing Agency | Social Media Marketing Business So, it is essential to safeguard your clients from fraud.

The most used method of payment is PayPal as well as credit card. Some people prefer to pay in cash. If you receive a request such as this, don't be shy about the request. It is best to inquire about the motive behind it in order to let them know you are concerned about their issues.

It is easy to jump directly from here into the price and package section, if operating an Digital Marketing Agency | Social Media Marketing Business or other kind of business. If you're a freelancer and you are a freelancer, you must include a professionally written blog on your website. It serves as an online portfolio for the Digital Marketing Agency | Social Media Marketing Business. It gives potential clients an opportunity to take an in-depth look at your manner before they decide to hire your services. The people love watching videos since they are more entertaining than reading text. If you can, make sure to include some videos on the services you provide on your site.

Strategy for marketing and sales

Market strategies are the initial step that business owners need to consider to determine how the company will compete and thrive within their industry. It includes products, pricing and promotion distribution channels, as well as other elements that are essential in determining the company's success or success or. Since sales are the primary source of income of your business and your business, it is imperative to be aware of the way each aspect of your market strategy affects the sales. This will determine how you'll find and communicate with potential customers.

Also, this is the time in which you begin to create your business's model by using the marketing strategies you employ. Social media is an essential component of any digital marketing strategy however it shouldn't be considered as an extra-nothing. The thinking process behind creating a plan for social media is not limited to using social media to drive customers to your website, rather it should be focused on the direction you would like those customers and leads to go once when they visit your site.

The marketing plan you create is the foundation of your business plan. The first step to developing an effective strategy is to comprehend the motivations behind the customer's behavior. To increase sales, it is essential to be aware of their needs and the ways your business can help them by offering offerings or products. If you understand what your clients want they want, you'll be able to reach at them. Through keeping track of the behavior of your customers on a regular basis, and comparing it to your own sales statistics You can make changes to your plan as required.

The most efficient method to reach consumers is via online advertisements. Marketers constantly seek out ways to advertise their services or products through the fast-growing arena in digital marketing. A well-conceived approach to digital marketing is essential for the success and growth of any company. If you are looking to increase leads or boost sales via online channels, you must have an approach that will give the most chance for success.

Public relations can enhance your image for your business in an industry sector, aid you attract new customers and enhance your image. For success using a strategy for public relations you must understand what is the basis of the news and how your business can fit to it. It is also essential to have a strategy to achieve these goals by balancing risks and opportunities aspects. We'll decide whether or not your business is the right fit with PR based upon the overall business model, product and services, demographics, and many other elements.

After you have completed a thorough study of the market you will be able to create a compelling branding strategy that will give your business a distinctive voice in its field and with consumers. To achieve this it is essential to identify the distinctiveness of your company and how it is positioned in the market and discover the platforms that can help you communicate your message in a way that is effective.

When you have a clear idea of your market segment You must be sure that they know your business exists and that it is an option they can consider. The marketing process involves creating relationships with your customers via print, online and social media channels. To achieve this goal you have to work within the confines of your budget and also focus on the long-term growth and profits. If you take the time to study your customers to enhance their experience with your customers which can help to build loyalty for your business in the near future.

Social media is an effective method to improve the image of your company through live interactions with existing and prospective customers and clients. A strong social media presence can boost your business' image in the market and eventually bring in new clients. Making a plan to implement social media is crucial to the success. Sharing information on a variety of popular social media platforms isn't enough. You also have to build relationships with your customers via engagement with the community, as well as providing helpful information.

Making a successful digital marketing strategy can be difficult for many businesses particularly those who are just beginning to learn about the field. You must establish social media goals and know the role your company plays in the ever-changing world. Through establishing relationships with those who share your content through social media platforms, and gaining trust from the public, you can dramatically increase sales for your business.

Facebook marketing is efficient in increasing sales and creating leads.

From a business point perspective, Facebook was the first to allow Pages for catalogs, films and celebrities, businesses, and other organizations (including non-profits) and gave them an area on its website where information can be shared with customers. Marketers don't have to wait for media to announce a news story about their products or services. When they create a Facebook Page you have full control over the way that their message is displayed via their own channels of media. Making engaging content for this website can help you draw new customers and increase sales.

Constant Contact provides an extensive listing of marketing via social media options to help you increase the visibility for your company.

Social media is now an increasingly popular method to make your business visible and interacting with customers and promoting new products and services. Constant Contact provides a wealth of assistance for business and individuals trying to get more customers via social media.

40

Services include monitoring for mentions that mention the company's name and also responses to posts on Facebook, LinkedIn, Twitter, Google+, YouTube and various other platforms. Constant Contact also offers social media marketing to aid you in getting new customers, increase sales, and build your brand using a variety of tools, including blogs and Facebook pages. Google+ pages, or LinkedIn corporate pages.

Utilizing social networks as a digital marketing has grown increasingly important as it provides consumers with an effective and reliable platform to get information about products, and for interaction to the company. It can take forms of discussion or sharing of content on their platform in addition to traditional techniques like mailing direct mail, or using email to offer digital media support to incident response programs. The continuous utilization of the social media channels aids to the creation of connections and dialogue which other types of marketing communications cannot achieve. With the growing utilization of social media channels, businesses should have a deliberate and consistent approach to their use in order to increase their competitive advantage.

The online reputation management (ORM) Services provide companies with a method to monitor online conversations regarding their company and its product or service. Businesses can choose the content that appears on these sites. If the business is a company, their reputation is managed and secured by using on-line ORM services to make sure that any content that could be damaging is removed prior to it reaching the internet community. This kind of service comprises monitoring services and social media management services and website analysis work and reputation restoration.

The posting of information on different popular social media platforms will help in the success of your company. The plan is to establish several accounts, and then start posting regularly on these platforms which are relevant to your business. The content you share must be engaging and interesting enough to keep your followers coming to your site to read more. With these channels, you'll be able to engage with your intended audience and showcase your services in a manner that is easily digestible.

Management and organization

What is the difference between management and organization? The management and organization of a business are linked to hierarchy the process and communication methods, roles, and goals.

Business analysis: analyze your company from the point of the customers' or clients. Business audits are the process of analysing and improving business decision-making to improve customer happiness and share. It it is based on determining strengths and weaknesses, based on the quantitative and qualitative aspects.

Organized chart of the structure and the administration of an business is a function of the hierarchy, processes and communication channels, as well as the responsibility. Hierarchical structures are central to all companies, from successful large corporations that have "the big boss" or the CEO as its leader down to smaller family-run businesses where everyone is involved to come up with solutions.

Basic structure: Projects, business departments, and projects according to industry; according to the location. In the hierarchy of a company it has three different levels that comprise the top level of management (CEO) middle management (i.e. department managers) and front-line workers or employees at the workstations producing products and services to the business. Project managers manage the tasks and may also be an orderly structure of departments, e.g. sales and customer service, marketing and accounts and so on. Each with its own manager or head.

A lot of companies have internal staff that work in two or more domains (e.g. it is possible to witness this at IT firms). Hierarchies have to be effective and efficient for the smooth operation of any business. This means that employees at all levels need to be able to coordinate their tasks efficiently (e.g. employees in customer service are aware of sales goals and sales targets, etc.).

Business operations The way in which the business is operated each day, i.e., accounting and payroll as well as personnel.

Process of business: how companies are organized in their daily activities that must be accomplished. This refers to the process of completing an task or an activity such as from beginning to finish, and also includes the decision-making in each stage.

Quality control Control of quality: Standards, inspection and evaluation, as well as improvements to processes via evaluations and feedback. Management of business processes (BPM) can be described as a methodical process to enhance and improve business processes. BPM involves the study of the current process in order to identify bottlenecks and weaknesses creating new processes and then implementing them.

Business intelligence is a broader effort to ensure continuous improvements in operational efficiency via gathering data, data analysis and making decisions. Business intelligence is also used to make strategic choices. It's mostly a set of techniques and tools companies can employ to analyse business data to discover potential opportunities, trends or threats and also plan to plan for the coming years (e.g. forecasts of trends or profile of customers). Business intelligence is a combination of processes, people technology and processes to enhance the decision-making process within an company. Business intelligence includes areas such like business performance management (BPM) and Customer relationship management (CRM) and marketing analytics.

Financial analysis: Examine the financial health of a business. This includes the investment strategy and debt repayment schedule and profitability indicators. Financial control involves measuring actual results against forecasts and plans to approved standards. Financial control involves the study of the value of time (i.e. the calculation of the NPV or amortization period of a loan) and also studying profits and budgets against actuals (i.e. variation analysis).

Organizational culture: It is the unspoken guidelines and practices, behavior as well as the attitudes and values of the organization that influence the way employees perform their work. The organization's culture is an essential tool for gaining competitive advantages. Culture is the assumption of how to best organize resources and people to meet the business goals, as well as the shared vision, mission and strategies (i.e., "being all for one")

CSR stands for Corporate Social Responsibility. (CSR) is the belief that businesses for profit must be held accountable to be ethical and aid in economic growth in order to improve the standard of living of everyone involved. CSR principles must be applied in everyday activities, business procedures, and corporate behaviour. It is about transparency to all parties involved including employees, suppliers, as well as the general public. Corporate social responsibility focuses on:

1.) Protection of the environment (e.g. pollution, resource depletion or climate change)

2.) Justice for the social (e.g. human and child rights as well as diversity issues as well as gender equity)

3.) Development that is sustainable (i.e. growth in economics that is not harmful to the future generations or the environment)

Environmental management is a set of the guidelines and procedures that safeguard the environment, such as emission, energy consumption, as well as waste disposal. EIA stands for environmental impact analysis. (EIA) is a term used to describe methods for assessing the environmental impacts of a proposed action prior to its implementation.

Environmental Management System (EMS) is a set of strict guidelines and standards designed to assist companies in managing their environmental performance. Systems for environmental management, specifically, ISO 14001 certification guarantees that the company is in compliance with environmental regulations or the best practices.

Social media marketing refers to marketing online via social media platforms like Facebook, Twitter, etc. These sites are generally geared toward consumers and provide users with a variety of ways to connect , including blogs, groups, pictures and videos. In addition, they usually include social networking functions which allows users to connect and connect with others by using pre-set guidelines. Marketing via social media is among the most efficient ways for businesses to sell their products or services on the internet because it gives insight into the customers' motivations and their interests. Social media channels can be utilized to collect market intelligence on competitors and also influence the behavior of consumers and public opinions. Tools for marketing on social media are Twitter, Facebook, YouTube, Google Plus, Pinterest and many more.

Digital marketing is a type of marketing strategy which is focused on improving every aspect of customer service with regard to digital technologies like smartphones as well as the web. It includes services like email marketing as well as search engine optimization or social media advertising. It also encompasses services that are designed to improve online shopping like pricing comparison software, generating web traffic via the use of search engine marketing (SEM) etc.

A campaign that is an email brief message or advertisement that is delivered via e-mail for the benefit of an organization. Campaigns using email are utilized for direct communications with clients

(e.g. to announce the services or products of the business or announce special deals or promote a new service or product, etc.)

Content marketing is the process of the creation and distribution of helpful content (blog posts informational guides, guides etc.).) to establish trust with customers and keep them coming back to the website of the company. Content Marketing is more about relationship-building than direct sales pitches. Content marketing can be described as video or image blogs and podcasts, press release ebooks, webinars, and press releases. It's a long-term investment to build brand recognition and trust, not a returns in return on investments (ROI).

Social media marketing refers to online marketing strategies that are conducted via social media platforms like Facebook, Twitter, etc. They are typically geared towards the consumer and provide users with a variety of ways to connect , including posts, groups photographs, videos, and group posts. They also often have the social networking feature which allows users to connect and connect with others with predefined guidelines. The use of social media for marketing has been among the most efficient ways to market products or services on the internet because it offers insight into consumers' motives and preferences. Social media channels can be utilized to gather market information about competitors, as well as to influence public opinions. Tools for marketing on social media comprise Twitter, Facebook, YouTube, Google Plus, Pinterest, and others.

Chapter 3: Create Your Site

How to set up WordPress

An Introduction to WordPress Blogging: Discover How to set up the best free Blogging Platform for Your Company!

How can I create an online blog using WordPress?

Why WordPress? What is the most suitable blogging platform for 2015 for me? What can I do to determine which blogging platform for free and WordPress themes would fit my company the most?

How do I get started with my blog using WordPress and what necessary plugins do I need to install to begin?

This article will cover everything! When you finish this article, you'll have everything you need to start blogging using WordPress!

How do we create a free WordPress Blog?

There are a variety of options available for blogs that are free, including Wordpress.com that has some limitations. You can also pay for a monthly or annual cost, but I don't suggest it because there are better alternatives that WordPress for blogs, such as the self-hosted wordpress.org, blogspot.com.

How do I obtain my Domain Name?

The domain is your site's web address. Selecting a suitable domain name is a crucial element in creating your blog. It is important to pick a domain that is a reflection of what you do however, it shouldn't be so broad that it means any thing. This is why the WordPress company plan can help you through the process of setting up an domain name and website. You can make use of an unpaid version wordpress.com or purchase self-hosted WordPress with an premium theme.

What's different between using WordPress and buying a self-hosted website?

The main benefit of hosting your own site is that you be in complete control of the layout, features and plug-ins that are available on your website. You could also earn money from your website through the use of affiliate links or ads. You can make money from blogs on BlogSpot. BlogSpot blog, too.

How do I create an entirely self-hosted WordPress blog?

If you want to set your blog, follow these steps.

1. Incorporate the blog's name at the top of the right to let people be able to identify it.

2. Install the Theme (free or paid)

3. Install all your widgets and plugins

4. Make sure you fill out your About Me page with the most important details

5. Blog about something you've written on your site You can write whatever you like! Be sure to write high-quality content that readers will find fascinating.

6. Create your first blog post!

7. Repeat until you are happy with the design of your blog

How can I increase my blog's traffic?

The easiest method to gain new visitors is to make other websites, blogs or social media accounts connect to your site. The more sites link back to you the better, as new visitors will come across it and will likely visit your site.

How do I find other websites to link with my website?

The first thing you need to do is create quality unique content for your blog. It can be difficult at times however it's something bloggers have to do. In the next step, you must develop a website plan for your website to let people are aware of the pages that exist and where they're located on the site.

How important is my blog's homepage?

The most important page of the WordPress website is your homepage. It's because it's to get the largest volume of visitors. It is not enough to concentrate on writing content that's good on this blog, but ensure that your blog's homepage is optimized. This involves using the most popular keywords and including a hyperlink to another website in order for more back links to your site.

How do I use social media?

If you're running an WordPress blog there are numerous ways to use social media to help your blog. It is recommended that you be a member on all of the most popular social media platforms such as Facebook, Pinterest, Twitter as well as Google+.

You should make use of these websites for the purpose of using them inform people about your site, and also to increase the number of visitors to your site. Also, you should frequently make sure to update these accounts with new content on your WordPress website. This will increase the number of visitors to your site via search engines.

WordPress FAQ

Create a FAQ page on the FAQ page on your WordPress blog. This can help you answer questions people might have about your business that they may not be able to use your contact page. It could also be an opportunity for your customers and readers to find more information on your products and services you offer. I would recommend using the WPFAQ plugin since it offers more options than the standard WordPress FAQ plugin.

How do I create a blogroll?

The blogroll can be described as a list of hyperlinks to other blogs you enjoy or find useful, sometimes referred to as "favorite hyperlinks." It is also possible to use it to create an affiliate page on behalf of other services or products that you utilize.

To include a blogroll in your WordPress website, you must first sign up for an account with WP-ListWizard and then add the plugin to your WordPress website. The page to add hyperlinks is found in Settings > WP-Listwizard Settings.

How do I contact you?

I can be contacted by phone: (248) 555-5555, email: web [at] digitalmarketingagency.co , web site:

https://www.digitalmarketingagency.co/ Facebook.

How do you handle returns?

We have a return and exchange policy that is easy If you're still not entirely satisfied with your purchase contact us and we'll process a full reimbursement to the original method that you used to pay within thirty days. This policy was never and isn't meant for people who've decided that they don't want it anymore , or have made a change of mind. It's risk-free.

What are the advantages from using your service over other companies' services that offer similar services?

There are numerous advantages of choosing our service over other companies. The reason we are able to provide such affordable rates and still provide a top product is because we have cut out all costs associated with overhead through offering design and hosting services on Cloud servers. Our infrastructure lets us provide resources at times of need so that during high traffic periods, there aren't any delays or interruptions.

Chapter 4: Attracting Clients

The clients are the heartbeat for any agency that is digital. Many marketing agencies depend on their clients to generate revenues. You won't be able to sustain company if there are no customers and the only way to increase your client base is by having a successful strategic plan for digital marketing. This strategy for digital marketing will help you get clients as well as keeping the ones you have.

The most basic of all the digital marketing plan must consist of at least three components: reaching out to new clients and maintaining existing business and increasing sales. Each of these parts should include distinct ways in which the company will achieve its objectives.

The primary goals of the company within this segment of the online marketing strategy is to present its products and services and attract the attention of. The most effective way to achieve this is to establish an online presence, which is achieved by having an online presence and social media accounts or blogs. It is equally important that prospective customers are aware of the location of your company as well as your contact information.

The other part in the online marketing strategy is to keep the existing business, that's every relationship with clients after introduction. The primary goals of this portion is to keep clients who are already working with you to ensure they're happy with your service and introduce new services or products that might be beneficial to them. It's also essential to get regular business from clients through keeping the good connection you've made with them.

This section of the digital marketing plan is to make new sales. This means that a company is trying to promote its products or services to prospective customers. The primary goals of this segment are to make sure that all client requirements are fulfilled and that there is satisfaction of the customers. The goal of bringing in new sales is always an important business objective, whether that's the acquisition of new clients or selling to existing clients who already work with the agency.

In the end, it's crucial that the digital marketing plan should take into account any legal responsibilities and the compliance requirements of governments across the various areas of their offerings. It is also crucial to establish guidelines and education to promote ethical behavior, including security of personal data, personal data protection and privacy.

This is only sketch of the digital marketing program however, you must be aware that it could become more or less complex dependent on the company and its objectives. Digital marketers can assist you throughout the process and will advise you on how to make your website more effective and boost sales via the internet.

The art of attracting clients

The method by which clients are acquired is via word-of mouth. There are many aspects to think about if would like your clients to be satisfied with the services that you offer. From the very beginning, it must be the goal of every company to not just attract clients, but also to keep them.

Companies can achieve this and be more successful when they implement methods of digital marketing. Digital marketing can aid a business develop because it is the most effective method of communication. With this kind of power, companies can connect with prospective customers.

The initial step in the digital advertising strategy should be to get online visibility. That means your business must have an online presence with a website you can promote to your prospective clients. Additionally, you should have social media accounts to ensure that when people type in your interests, you'll show up at the top of search results.

It is crucial that customers who come across your site appropriate and useful to their requirements because in the event that they don't, there is no reason to have a any business relations with them. Customers will be able to ask questions about your company and it's okay to will find answers to their queries. If you're honest you will establish trust with your client which will result in more sales.

There must also be the strategy to brand your business so that whatever service or product you provide to your clients your company's name will be connected to the image they think of in their heads. A well-known brand can help build confidence between your customer and your company.

The proper digital marketing strategy will ensure that you are on the right course to meet your objectives and achieve them before the deadline.

What is the best way to Close The Deal

The primary goal of closing an agreement is to convince clients to act. If the customer isn't doing something, you'll never be able to keep them as a client. This is the reason your plan should involve getting customers to take decisions.

As mentioned earlier, customers are always asking questions about your business , and they'll be able to find answers on your site. It should be simple to understand and read for them, so they won't have any issues getting around the site.

Clients also require reasons to choose your business over your competitors. This is when you can make use of promotional offers to lock in the sale, but that doesn't mean that you don't need to be attentive following that point. Call tracking can give you the opportunity to keep your client and focus on creating a loyal client.

Inbound Marketing

Inbound marketing beginning by understanding how your people are searching for youto begin. It is important to know what customers are saying about your competitors , and what they're saying about your company.

Inbound marketing means bringing clients to visit your website, where you are able to still assist them and make customers feel happy, even if this is the first time they've heard about your business. It is important to use inbound marketing if you wish to keep customers and keep coming back. The procedure should be planned to achieve these goals.

Inbound marketing can develop strategies that will make your website appear on search engines with the most appropriate keywords. Additionally, you should have campaigns on social media created so that when customers come across information about your company they are able to engage with it and then share the information with their social media followers. This is only one of numerous strategies available to assist you in reaching your objectives.

In the end, if you're looking to create an effective digital marketing strategy then you must ensure that your plans be effective and will help your company be noticed. It is essential to create the perfect plan for each client to ensure they can become regular clients. Your clients must be satisfied with the business relationship they have with you, and this happens when they're seeing excellent results.

Chapter 5: Recruit The Best People

The ideal scenario is that every business should have a strong brand name that has individual branding of the proprietor of the business. You must be able to make an impactful impression about your company. In order to hire the best individuals, you have to be clear about your communication and understand the exact thing you're looking for. Allow other candidates to give their opinions prior to talking with your potential candidates.

Your task is to ensure that applicants are prepared so that you are able to determine which best fits your business. It's important that you go with your instincts when you are hiring employees. If you don't feel a candidate seems to be the right fit, then they're probably not the right fit for you. Make sure that they're speaking about the right topics - your offerings and the services you are able to offer your customers.

The company culture is also crucial when hiring the right employees. It is a good idea to have someone arrive and share their opinions on the corporate culture they'd like to adopt if they accepted the job. So, there's no surprises later in the future.

Freelancer vs In-House Employee

There always are pros and cons for either of these choices. You must decide which option is best for your business over the long term. Internal employees can cause difficult at times but it's important to know that they're more involved in the company than freelancers are. They have a better understanding of the activities that take place outside of work hours. There's also a certain amount of trust you can trust them with.

Freelancers can be employed lower costs than employees in the company, which is why they're great for clients who are just starting out and are working at a part-time basis. They'll require a larger budget to pay other freelancers , or in-house workers, and should their business grow and they grow, then perhaps they'll consider hiring an employee full-time.

The pros and cons are there to each option, but you must to determine which is the best fit for your business.

When you decide to take on internal employees, it's usually an ongoing position. It is a responsibility for their families as well, and there's a greater amount of pressure when you hire someone else than those that can manage their own lives. Additionally, you'll face a number of legal concerns when you employ an employee because they're an extension of your company. However freelancers are employed for projects that are short-term, and you're not accountable for their work. However, the trade-off is that you're able to recruit more freelancers than employees, if the project proves to be an enormous success.

In general hiring employees in-house is likely to be better than hiring freelancers as you'll have longer-term strategies for your business. You may not be able to employ as many employees like if you employ freelancers but it's well worth it since they're trustworthy and loyal.

It can be a great temporary solution, but in the long-term hiring employees is the best most effective option.

In this article, I'll discuss how it's different to employ freelancers, rather than employees in-house. As I've said it is possible to hire freelancers at a lower cost, however, they may not be aware more about business like in-house employees are. This could be a problem for companies that are just beginning and results aren't as you thought they would be. Freelancers will take every penny that you've got for them and may even quit after finishing the project because they don't have anything left to their families.

In my opinion, freelancers are beneficial for big businesses as well as companies who already have an online presence. Because their reputations are at stake, they'll be more focused on the task. If your business has only one person running it the freelancers might not be the right choice.

If you are hiring freelancers or employees, you must have patience. You'll have to be flexible with regards to deadlines as they could take longer than you anticipated them to complete so keep the idea in your head.

How to Find Employers

It's difficult to find suitable employees because you don't have a clue which kind of employees are working for your company. You can consult with people or look online to see if there are an abundance of people interested in joining your business. If you don't find anything and you're not sure, you might consider advertising on the internet or locally so that you can reach out to a large market.

Of course, you'll need to be able to demonstrate the right qualifications for your company in order to be able to employ more than one employee. If your business doesn't have an established reputation as it's brand new it's likely that there won't be as competitive when employing new employees.

If you are hiring employees on an extended period of time make sure that they're capable of the task and that you be sure that they will do the job. How can your company develop into something bigger If you don't have employees who are capable of helping you out?

If they're skilled employees, that doesn't mean that they'll join your business. You'll have to offer them something higher than the typical salary to make them more likely to be willing to join your company. In this way, your business has a greater likelihood of success, especially when dealing with workers.

It is important to know that if you employ someone who is not qualified for the position or doesn't desire to take on the task and you don't know why, there's no way to fix it. It is not a good idea to hire people who don't want to do the job or else you'll find yourself in a worse position than you were before.

If you're in search of employees, you should take into consideration the way they operate or how effective the team works when they're working together. The personalities of the employees will be significant as they can influence how they tackle future projects. If you aren't able to find people who are able to work well together, then it's going to be difficult for your business to progress.

Paying employees and how they are How Employees Are Managed

The most crucial aspects you need to take care of is properly manage your workers to ensure that there aren't any issues in or out of the workplace. In this way, your company can advance without any problems.

The majority of workers want an income that is sufficient for them to live their lives, so providing lower-than-average wages won't be enough. Freelancers are less experienced and are willing to be lower wages, however it is essential to hire people who can perform the task correctly. It is also essential to make sure that your employees work in a safe and secure environment, so they aren't injured.

Employees are easily discouraged when you aren't treating them fairly. Make sure only the most qualified employees are employed by your company and be willing to offer them a higher salary in the event that you wish to keep them for more than one year.

It's impossible for your business to grow if it doesn't have people working together towards the same goals. If your employees are engaged in their job, they'll be able to produce results for the business that will allow it to grow. Of course, you must be sure that they are doing their best, as there is no need for employees that don't work hard for their wages.

If you're able to manage your team, your business will expand faster because they'll be a part of a team and complete the task within the timeframe. They will be able to meet deadlines more quickly than if working on your own, so you should make sure to take advantage of this to your advantage.

If you have a team who is capable of working in a team, your company will increase its growth rate because everyone is striving to achieve the identical objective. This kind of work cannot be done by one person , therefore it's recommended to have more than one person.

Chapter 6: Market Research

Market research is among the most important factors prior to beginning a business. It assists in identifying fundamental information about competitors' offerings and products. This will help you determine your strategy for winning over your competition by challenging their ideas with innovative strategies that are sure to bring the business you want to be successful.

Understanding the market

To accomplish this it is essential to stay up-to-date with the latest trends in the digital and offline world of business. If you conduct a thorough study it will allow you to see what your competitors are doing and can create more original strategies, ideas and strategies to outdo them. Some of the things you can accomplish here include:

Learn about the needs of consumers and their desires: This is the most crucial aspect to be aware of. It is important to understand what customers expect from their products and services, so that you can get an understanding of how your company will be able to win their trust.

If you are aware of all these factors, you'll be better equipped to develop an effective strategy for how your business will stand out and make it more accessible to your market.

Research methods

Primarily research: As of this point, you're aware of how essential for you to do market research prior to beginning a business. You may conduct an initial analysis on your own or seek the assistance of experts in the area. In addition it is also necessary to conduct some sort of research in the beginning. This could include:

Discussions in focus groups (FGDs) The method involves a small group with a few people in which you discuss and receive feedback on your service or product idea. It is recommended to ask them questions that directly relate to the product or service that you plan to provide. The benefit of this is that it's cost-effective.

Primarily data gathering: This is the most popular and sophisticated type of research in which you look over the information collected and find options for your company.

Second research next stage of market research is second analysis, or evaluation. This means you're using the available sources in the market to find out more about your competition.

If, for instance, you plan to open a restaurant, then go to several restaurants in your local area and observe their operation. You'll notice that they employ different ways to run their businesses; by the menu they offer and pricing strategies, to the products or services they offer (i.e. how they market their goods) and the location where it is situated and more. These are just a few aspects you should be considering. This will assist you in determining your company's business plan and how you can outdo your competitors in winning the hearts of customers.

Pricing strategies

Once you know what customers want Pricing strategies follow which is among the top crucial factors in managing an online business. It is important to first define your market segment which could be either global or local.

Then, you need to figure out the most appropriate price for your service or product The price will be determined by:

Targeted pricing is a method which allows your company to provide the most unique and specific range of services and products to satisfy the needs of clients.

Mark-up pricing: This is the time to include a certain amount of cost to your services or products and thus allow you to make more money. Marketing strategies

After you've learned about your competitors in the field and what they have to provide, it's now time to take on them using an effective marketing plan that will definitely draw potential customers to your company.

What you must do is:

Advertising: It's likely to be the highest-cost element of any company, but it could be a great way to earn more money in return. If done correctly, it can give you an advantage over competitors and help ensure that your product or service is popular with people in the marketplace. Advertising can take place in various ways However, the most well-known option is to use printed ads, which are published in the top newspapers and magazines.

Planning for Marketing: It's an excellent idea to develop the marketing plan of your company. But don't be concerned, this does not mean that you'll employ it as a plan for every single thing you'll carry out. It's a summary of the marketing strategies you'd like explore and when. It assists you in keeping on top of your company's goals and ways you can reach them.

Acquisition of clients If everything goes according to plan then there's the chance that lots of customers will be interested in the product you offer or. If you're a restaurant, you could expect to see large lines of patrons waiting in line outside to enter.

A Risk Management Strategy: To prevent loss and risks in your the business process, It is essential to develop a risk management strategy. This should include a variety of actions to protect against unplanned mistakes that could cause harm to your business. It also includes the possibility of becoming involved in legal matters and accidents, theft by employees and other such issues.

Find your target audience

If you don't take care of this, it could cause an enormous impact on your business if you allow it slip. Another thing you need to be considering is determining who is likely to purchase the product you offer or services, the audience you want to target. There are three methods to knowing who your target customer is:

Geographic market segmentation involves the division of the general market into different groups based on the location they reside. This gives you a more precise information about the primary customer.

Demographic segmentation is like the other option, with the exception that it differentiates prospective clients according to their gender, age and social class as well as their education level and the list goes on.

Segmentation of services and products In this case, you'll further segment your customers based on the item or service they wish to purchase. If, for instance, you have a clothing store the segmentation will allow you to identify who is formal and who is more comfortable in casual clothes.

Setup for E-commerce: If you're looking to let potential buyers purchase things online from your site, then you be aware that setting up an E-commerce business setup will require more than simply purchasing the account.

It is, however, about the creation and maintenance of your website and will require experts to assist even if you're not technologically proficient. Many people see shopping online as a cheaper alternative , but it's contingent on the kind of business you're in. If you're in a competitive field or you're selling products that need an enormous amount of money to make to make, the equilibrium between quality and price is difficult to keep particularly if your primary customer base is solely online.

Support for customers: This isn't part of your marketing plan however it's still vital to think about this. In the end, your customers need some kind of contact from you. If they do not receive any communication, they are likely to be irritated or annoyed. Therefore, ensure that your site has at a minimum an email address to contact you with inquiries or feedback.

The name of a Digital Marketing Agency must be simple to remember: Make sure you choose the name of your business that is simple to remember. It can benefit not only you but also your clients who might refer you to others in the future.

An Digital Marketing Agency should be simple: You should not have to have a lengthy name for your company since it will be hard for customers to identify or pronounce.

A Digital Marketing Agency should be creative: Don't just go with the flow and settle for something like DigitalMarketingExpert, Inc.; it's better that you have your unique twist in your business names such as Digital Marketer or Digital Marketing. It's crucial the way it represents you company and is easily recognized by the public, so be sure to choose one that is distinctive.

Find your competitors' target and how to locate them: Before starting your own Digital Marketing Agency, make sure you research your competition. This will assist you determine the strengths and weaknesses of their marketing strategies to help you do more effectively than they do. It is also important to understand the reasons they're doing so well. After all imitation is the best kind of flattery. employ the same approach to be better than them.

Check their websites There is an overview of your prospective competitors on popular search engines directories for business, yellow pages. You can even direct contact them and they will forward you their brochures of sales.

Find out what's unique about each competitor: After you've gathered the information of every competitor, you must to determine what's unique about each of them. This will help you understand the reason they're so successful on the market and how you can defeat them at your own level. If, for instance, your competition has created an even better website than you do and is a better website, that's something you can improve on , too.

What industry are you a Digital Marketing Agency in? The first thing to do is find out what industry your business operates in. If it's a generic word, then it's not going to provide you with an advantage over your competitors. Instead choose something that is more specific, such as "designing and creating websites for small companies" and "specializing with SEO solutions". If you're looking to expand your offerings the scope of your business, it's best to investigate a different field. For instance, if you're selling car parts online it's more effective than going with the trend and call you an "online marketing business" Do something unique instead.

Which strengths do you have? You must identify your strengths and be focused on them. Then, you can use this to benefit your competition. For instance, if you're a skilled designer but your competitors do not have one, be sure to keep your strengths. By doing this they'll know that you're an expert in the field.

What's distinctive that you have in what makes you stand out from other Digital Marketing Agency? If you're confident that you've got the most effective marketing plan in your field ensure that you highlight that fact by coming up with a catchy slogan or tagline that differentiates your company from the rest. If, for instance, you're offering a superior analysis that other companies don't, then inform them about it. They'll surely be amazed by your expertise and skills.

What is your agency's most important advantages? If you want to find out the greatest feature of your company whether it's due to their expertise in advertising, designing or any other thing, utilize that as an advantage over your competition. If you know what makes your company distinct from others and then you can create your own niche market that will attract an even bigger number of customers.

What benefits will your customers receive by working together with you as a Digital Marketing Agency? What your company is doing and how to accomplish it isn't enough. it. You need to know why clients should pick your product instead of the competition. For instance, if you're an excellent web designer but your rival is also, what is the difference between them one another? You must consider your business from the customer from their perspective to understand what they're searching for.

What level of education and experience does you and your Digital Marketing Agency team have? You must be aware of the skills they can do and the amount of knowledge they'll bring to the company. If you're looking for your company to be among the top in its field, then ensure that the staff who work for your company are capable of doing this. For instance, if, for example, you're planning to become an SEO specialist but you don't know how to use the most recent software available for it and you're not sure how to do it, that's something you must do your best to improve.

Chapter 7: Branding And Scaling Strategies

When you have a clear idea of the nature of your business and what you can do to make it successful first, you'll need to determine how you can distinguish yourself from your competitors. For instance, if you're a newly-established web design firm, determine ways in which your company will be able to expand in the near future, and what branding concepts you can think of.

How do you market your company? A crucial thing to think about when conducting business is how be able to promote your business's image, and it all begins with branding. For instance, if you're planning to start an online design company and you want to create an identity and slogan that can be used to promote the brand. The right branding strategy can help you distinguish yourself from other businesses and, even if you're just starting out the brand you choose to represent will be well-known to other people.

The Structure of Branding

The specific branding requires a structure for properly branding your business. For instance, if you're thinking of creating a website design company that you are planning to establish, you must be able to:

What is the name of your organization? It is essential for your business to be memorable and catchy. name that is able to be shared across the entire community. You can create your brand name distinctive that is memorable or choose to base it on the field you intend to target. If, for instance, your company is focused on Web design and development, "Web Design Agency" is a great name.

What are you going to do to promote you Digital Marketing Agency? Whatever you think your company is, it's not going to suffice to make you noticed without the means to market your business. For instance, if you're thinking of starting an online marketing company but you don't know where or how to advertise your offerings, it's going to be a complete wasted of your time.

How can you create a way to make the Digital Marketing Agency stand out? After you've found ways to market your company, you must discover ways to distinct from rest. If, for instance, you're a specialist in web design however your competition is an expert in web design and your strategy must be focused on making sure that your company stand out. It can be done by offering superior services and superior customer service as compared to your competition.

What are the long-term objectives for your Digital Marketing Agency? It is essential in a position to think ahead and plan your company's in the future to get an concept of what you'll accomplish within the next few months. For instance, if you're thinking of starting an agency for web design within the next few weeks you should think about the long-term goals you'll be able to achieve within 6 months and one year. The long-term goals could be whatever, but you must to be aware of the direction your business will take into the next few years.

What are the reasons You need A Brand Strategy

A strategy for branding can help you identify your company and get it noticed by the market. In the absence of a strategy for branding, then you're not sure how to present your company to potential customers.

How to Use the Brand Strategy To Use In Your Business

If you're thinking of coming up with a strategy for branding for your company, you should be focusing on the following aspects:

What's your objective?

There must be an individual or commercial motive to open your own company. If, for instance, you're entering this digital marketing company in order to earn more money, this is a personal motivation however If you're doing it since you're looking to contribute to your community that's an economic motive.

What's your goal?

After you've identified your reason to start the business, now you must think of somewhere between one and two phrases that define your goals for this organization. For example, if looking to open an online marketing business in order to contribute back to your community, and aid small businesses, your mission statement might be "If we can help small-scale businesses expand, they will result in more employment and bring more money into your community economy." This is merely an example of a mission, and it could be anything else.

What do you consider your core values?

After establishing an objective and mission statement, you must determine your core values. These values will define the fundamental characteristics of your company. For instance, if looking to open an online marketing firm that aims to offer small-scale businesses top-quality services, but also keep the prices reasonable, then your primary values could include "quality along with affordability."

What is your company's image going get noticed? It is important to ensure that you don't create an individual reason to start this company. It is also important to think about how others are going to perceive it once they come across the name. For instance, if your business is branded "Online Marketing Agency" the public might view the name negatively since they don't think it is a legitimate brand. This negative perception by creating distinctive names, such as "HubSpot Marketing Agency."

What is your company's strategy to be a part of your community?

Once you've decided what your business wants to be able to portray, you can now create the phrases that best reflect the character of your local community. For example, if looking to open an agency for marketing where high-quality service and affordability are essential, the most appropriate statements are "We would like to assist small-sized businesses expand" and "Our aim is to assist small-sized businesses connect with more customers."

How do you run your business?

It is essential to ensure that you've got a good understanding of the things your business does each day. For instance, if considering starting a marketing firm which will assist the community in their times in need, you should know what steps your company will take in the event of a catastrophe like the occurrence of a hurricane.

What are the best ways to run your company?

It is essential to be aware of the employees in this field and what they will be able to accomplish. For instance, if you're looking to start an online business that is run by at home, what are you planning to do to manage tasks like hiring new employees as well as signing contracts with clients and coordinating the financials?

What are you planning to do to enhance your community?

It is essential to create some strategies for how you'll give back to your local economy. For instance, if you're thinking of creating an online marketing company for small-sized businesses, you could consider setting the donation box so that local businesses can donate their surplus inventory. Then, you'll make use of the items to sell them on eBay and then donate the proceeds to the local community.

How do you promote your company?

It is essential to have some plans to get people to know about the business. For instance, if you're thinking of opening an online marketing company, then you can advertise the business through local advertisements in the local newspaper or social media as well as blogs online.

What can you do to improve your company?

After you've come up with the perfect name for your brand, a good mission statement or core values, statements that define your community, as well as an outline of the way you'll run your business, you'll should think of some goals for how you'll improve the efficiency of this business. If, for instance, you're considering starting an online marketing agency One of the best ideas could be to set monthly goals to increase the number of followers on social media and encouraging smaller businesses to engage your company.

Storytelling and position

After you've verified that your company is correctly depicted, you're now required to ensure that your business is properly placed. Positioning a business is accomplished by creating a compelling narrative about the company. For instance, if looking to open an online marketing agency dubbed "Online Marketing Agency" then some excellent stories could be "Our online marketing firm assists in growing the business of a small one by developing websites as well as social media pages and other content" as well as "If you're thinking of hiring an online marketing firm to assist your small business to grow without spending a large amount of money, get in touch with us."

The process of creating a compelling story takes time. You must focus on your unique selling points, as well as differentiating factors. If, for instance, you're thinking of opening an online marketing company, then customer service and communication are two of your distinct factors, just as you can help A Film Grow is an distinctive selling factor for short documentary films.

Do what you can do to spread the public aware of your company. You must ensure that your business is sustainable since we'll be creating an image that will inspire people to conduct business with this firm. The narrative must be concise, clear and contain the key elements of your company. It is essential to explain the worth you can offer your customers, because when they don't feel that the way, then they'll not employ you.

Chapter 8: Copywriting

What is Copywriting?

Copywriting is a kind of advertisement that uses texts to influence and convert readers into buyers. Consider it this way when you come upon an advertisement that caught your interest and led you to buy the item, then you've seen copywriting in action.

How do you write effectively? Copy?

One thing that all great copywriters share is the ability to create captivating headlines. Take one look at these two headlines:

"Making Money Online Guaranteed!" "Want to earn money online Doing what you love?"

Which headline was more successful in converting you? Both headlines are good copies but , based upon the information above 54% of respondents were more intrigued by that second one. This is due to headlines that are easy and concise (such such as "Want to Make Money Online While Doing Something You Do Best?") have been proven to convert better than more complicated headlines (such as "Making Money Online , Guaranteed! ").

Be aware of what you're selling

Before you begin writing the first draft, you should look over your product. If it's an SaaS product, how do you define what that means? If your company is an online marketing company What can you do to convince clients that hiring you will aid in the growth of their small business?

The answer is straightforward: break the product into its primary features and highlight the advantages. If you're an online marketing agency, is it possible to hire an employee from your business to assist? How quickly can they increase the size of the company?

Copywriting for marketing must focus on the following questions effectively so that leads come that aren't boring and boring. It's a science and an art that is its own since you must convince people to engage, which is the entire point of this piece.

Actual Copywriting

These are real reviews from actual clients who have been so thrilled by the company's efficiency and mission that they kept coming back to get more.

"I've been working to develop my business of making music for quite a while. I already had accounts on social media and could create some content there, but not enough as my fans have requested. This is why I decided to employ an online marketing agency to help me solve this problem. When I was researching on the internet, I came across Help A Film Grow and I reached out to the company. Engaging them to manage my social marketing through social media was one of the best decisions I've ever made. "

Make use of Power Words

Power words are one type of word that convinces people to engage in action. For instance the phrases "new", "proven" and "unique" are very popular with entrepreneurs because they want to convince their customers that the opportunities they are preparing for them are brand new untested, tested, and exclusive opportunities.

Copywriting Power Words

These are among the most well-known keywords employed in copywriting. We've grouped them into categories to make it easier for use:

Power Words That Communicate the value to the audience

These words of power can convince customers that your product is of real value even though they don't understand the exact nature of it.

Power Word The Power Word

Cheap copywriting can be used to make the customer feel that your product will save the consumer by not spending too much on a different service or product.

If, for instance, you're selling the SaaS tool, you can say that it's less expensive than alternatives available and, therefore, more appealing to prospective customers.

Power Word Power Word: Free

Free is a term that's proved to be a good way to market almost everything. If you're looking for an effective word to include in your marketing materials, consider this.

However, even in the event that the service or product doesn't come "completely" completely free offering "freebie" features such as the option of a trial for free is usually employed together with the words "free" for convincing people that the product is worth exploring.

Power Word: Guaranteed

This word of power has been proven time repeatedly to persuade readers to take action as they are convinced that the if something doesn't seem to be guaranteed, then it could be an ad.

The feeling of security to a great extent in putting your customers feel at ease since they aren't taking a risk with their money or other items when they purchase from you. The powerful word "guaranteed" is best only used with caution to create a greater impact.

The AIDA Model

AIDA is a type of model that is that is used for direct advertising to describe how consumers process information that could lead to making a purchase. For instance, if you read an article on the internet, your brain goes through the following stages:

Attention, Interest, Desire, Action.

People who are already paying focus are those who take the time to read an article, without scrolling away or clicking another link. They aren't paying attention simply because they're interested, instead, it's the reverse the other way around. They're interested because they already have their attention.

There are numerous variables that determine the likelihood that your target customers will be able to go through these steps until they reach the point when they decide to decide to take action. It is important to ensure that you tailor your marketing and content to their needs.

If you're writing copy to promote digitally, you have to get the attention of your customer first , before he or she becomes interested in your service or product. Once they're intrigued, you have to make a convincing argument about the reasons why they should decide to buy from you.

If they're convinced this is when the AIDA model comes to an end, but it also indicates that your copywriting is performing the job it should. But, it isn't enough since even if you've got them convinced to buy from you, some customers could still decide to change their mind when they think the risk of purchasing from you isn't worth it.

The result is that they will be abandoning your site and heading to a competitor's site rather. It's not enough to just persuading your audience. It is also essential to provide solid assurances that make users believe that they'll purchase from you with confidence.

This AIDA Model is the base for all efficient digital marketing piece even if you're making use of it to promote the tangible item or service. You can still apply this model when creating content particularly for informative content that you wish to get them to take action right away by clicking the links or providing their contact details in order to receive the brochure.

CTA Call To Action Call To Action

CTA or call to action CTA called a "call to action" is that is used to get readers to take action immediately. typically, it's represented as buttons, text links or graphics that are inserted into the text. It is essential to tell the user to the next destination by using your CTA.

Imagine CTAs as bridges to take your readers to the next destination. If you would like readers to leave a message be sure to inform them of where to go and how to accomplish it.

It is important to be clear regarding what the CTA is and if you're uncertain about the action you'd like your customer to perform, think about adding buttons such as "learn more", "click here", "find out more" or similar words.

Always utilize the power word "free" in any instance where you're educating your audience on an CTA or when discussing the benefits that your service or product offers. Don't forget that money is a powerful motivator because if people see that something they want to purchase is free, they're much more likely to purchase it rather than having to charge the customer for it.

When you are writing your content, make sure you take a look at the entire picture , and consider all the variables that may influence the outcome. It is important to consider the AIDA model is only one of them , but there are other factors in play, including how color psychology affects typography, color and many other aspects. Be aware that many people today access their information from social media platforms like Facebook and Twitter Therefore, you must ensure the content you post is optimised for those platforms in addition to the fact that most users will simply choose the first search result they find instead of looking for a different site that has better ranking.

Last but not least, remember to not be in the copywriting industry to benefit yourself. It is important to meet the expectations of your customers and be responsive to their needs and wants in addition.

Be aware of them when you're promoting an item or service by presenting an informative piece, or showing them an infographic. They're the ones who will devour the information and then pass it on to their family and friends and offer suggestions according to the content. Your customer is your top concern when working as a digital copywriter.

Chapter 9: Marketing On Instagram

Marketing for Instagram is similar with Facebook marketing. You'll need good content for Instagram to engage your viewers and encourage them to follow you.

Keyword Research: Keywords are the foundation of any search engine. It is therefore essential to include keywords when developing an effective social media marketing strategy. Discover what your customers' needs and design an image using these key words.

Plan: Develop every aspect of your content in order to present a picture of your business or product. It is best to have a strategy for marketing on social media and not rely on one social network just. You can get the most effective results by utilizing multiple social networks to enhance your marketing strategy online and boost sales.

What's Next?

Create a marketing strategy using valuable information. Develop a plan for marketing your product. Make sure that you stick to the plan. Make a plan to continue improving the social media strategy you use for marketing strategies, making sure that your message is clear and concise in each posting. Utilize all the knowledge you've gained about quality content creating as well as social media marketing and SEO. Keep in touch with your customers.

Posting Schedule

The posting schedule is created so that you update every two to three days on each site , and frequently. It is important to stay clear of the pitfalls of posting too frequently or too often that can hurt your engagement in the long run. This chart will guide you through how to publish with this method.

How to Grow on Instagram

Utilize these strategies to increase your reach your presence on Instagram with your company. Build followers, increase leads, and help customers! Every study has demonstrated how social networks are the most important factor in a business's growth throughout 2016 , and even beyond. It's evident that if you don't have an established presence on social media, you're losing prospective customers as well as sales. Marketing on social media can assist in this regard and more, so don't dwell in the past, but don't pay attention to the way your customers interact on the internet today.

These steps will assist you to build a solid social media strategy for Instagram and you'll be taught how to create an image that inspires people to be drawn to you and

Create your brand by interacting with your customers and inspiring others.

Connect with potential customers in order to help them find your business online. Don't put off building now! What's Instagram is all about? There are three main aspects of Instagram: personal, business and marketing. The most important aspect of Instagram is its marketing opportunities. Since big corporations and companies are beginning to utilize Instagram to market their products the app has seen a massive increase in popularity. It's now among the most popular social media applications by people of all different ages.

The purpose behind expanding your Instagram account Instagram is to create followers who will be following you. This makes advertising much easier since they are already familiar with your posts. In order to achieve this, you have to be able to convince people to follow your company on Instagram.

There are a variety of ways you can increase your reach on Instagram by putting together a sound marketing plan for social media. One of the most important things you need to think about is to take great pictures of your product. If you've got a popular Instagram account and your followers are loyal, they are likely to be attracted by your page due to the number of followers you have as well as the quality of your photos.

Social Media Marketing Strategy

It is recommended to use an image that is similar to the other images in order to maintain the same look across every posting on the social media advertising strategy. The best way to go is create a design for your brand and stay to it. If your posts are all identical, it will help establish consistency across the social media advertising strategy and makes people desire to follow you more as a result.

Instagram is also a great platform to receive feedback from customers who have already a great experience with your product. People will be more inclined to recommend your products to others if they enjoy the products a lot. Your customers can leave positive reviews and help you to see your growth through social marketing opportunities on social media.

Also, you should utilize hashtags on Instagram to draw more users to your page. Be careful not to use excessive hashtags, or you'll scare people away. To enhance the social media advertising strategy even more effective, you can integrate it your social networks with others to broaden your reach and increase market share.

Profile Overview

The Company Overview is a brief summary of what the business does and where it is situated.

Details can be included in bullet points at the bottom of this webpage, and also logos of clients or partners when appropriate.

Coverage Areas - List your primary areas of coverage here. Examples are: "We provide public relations services to small-sized businesses across the U.S." or "We offer public relations and marketing services to industrial and retail clients throughout in the United States"

Specialties - List your specialty here. Some examples include "Our experience is in working closely with non-profit organizations, start-ups and small companies to raise the awareness of their products or products or"; "We have a established track record of generating awareness of a broad range in products"; "We specialize in cross-media marketing strategies".

Industries You Serve - List the industries you service and the kind of businesses, companies or individuals with whom you collaborate. Examples are: "We specialize in serving small business owners who are internet-savvy and wish to maximize their exposure on the internet. "; "Our primary focus is working with clients that require to create awareness for an innovative product, idea, or brand."

Change to Business Account

The Instagram corporate account an essential tool for marketing on social media. It can help your business to market its the products and services you offer, and offer discounts to those who are following you on this channel. Set up your own Instagram business account following the steps listed below.

1. Search and choose "Business" among the list of options offered

Step 2: Select your profile for business. On the next page, it will require you to fill in details related to your company name, company's name, category and the location.

3. Step 4: have to input the contact details of your company, including the address, number of phone and so on. in the space provided.

You can also activate the check-in option by selecting it in the "Add features to your account" section. You must specify the hours you are available and what is available at the time . You can accomplish this by clicking"Details" or "Details" link.

The fourth step is that you must make sure to promote your business by putting in personal messages about your brand, business or product

Step 5: Upload your profile picture and the logo of your company and you're done right now.

Interacting with Instagram users

A Instagram business account can be utilized to interact with other users. You can begin a conversation with your followers in order to gain more interaction from them. Don't be shy about starting the conversation, but ensure that you're adding value by offering assistance or helpful tips to your people you follow.

Insights and Analytics

The Instagram business account can provide you with valuable information. It will let you know the number of people who follow your business, the amount of likes and comments posted on images, etc. It also provides information about ad impressions and pages viewed, traffic sources and much more in the section called "Insights. You can review the statistics on the Instagram business account on a daily basis but when your team members are who works for your brand they should perform this task to gain more interaction from users.

Service Offerings

You must list your services products to promote your business effectively. It's not required, but if you're seeking to increase your followers, it can aid in building a solid relationship with them. Within this area, make sure to include links to material that you already have on your blog or website and also keep updating the information on a regular basis to ensure that users can quickly access your company.

Content Strategy Plan

This Instagram business account can be used to share photos and videos related to your company. You must develop an overall strategy for content to gain more attention from your followers. This will help you determine what kind of content is most effective for your business and what your customers are seeking from you. It is just a matter of dividing the content into various categories like helpful, how-to guides special offers or discounts behind the scenes of commercial shootsetc. This type of content can help you gain more followers. It is important to post pictures and videos regularly and frequently because it will improve your engagement as well as improve interactions with your followers. Also, you should make use of hashtags frequently to gain visibility for your business within the community.

Chapter 10: The Facebook Ads

Facebook advertisements can help you gain more attention for your company. It is possible to target an audience according to demographics, interest and locations. This type of marketing aids to gain followers, likes and pageviews from individuals in addition to increasing visitors to your site or blog. If you're making use of Facebook ads to promote your business It is crucial to make sure you use a proper call-to-action in order to increase the number of clicks on your advertisements. Also, you must ensure that the images and images of your advertisements are interesting enough to draw attention of users. It is also essential to develop a budget for your advertisements as if you do not have a budget, it's extremely difficult to reach out to a huge number of people.

Learn more about Facebook ads to increase engagement for your company. It is also advisable to ask users to comment and like photos and provide feedback on the business. It is also important to be connected to the other Instagram users to build relationships with them. If you require assistance and assistance, then contact Instagram's Instagram support team through live chat, emails or by phone to obtain all the information regarding your account.

Facebook Ads Goals

Facebook ads assist in bringing traffic to your blog or website. It is important to choose the best target based on your business objectives of your company. It is essential to develop an effective plan for Facebook advertisements. If you're making use of the ads to increase the brand's recognition it is important to concentrate at reaching out to wide range of people and increasing their knowledge about your business.

The best thing to do is grow your social media following number. If you have an impressive number of followers, it's a good idea for people to join our group. Therefore, as increasing numbers of people begin following your account, the visibility of your brand will rise.

How can you get an incredibly high rate of engagement on Facebook ads?

It is recommended to try creating an Facebook advertisement that has an excellent engagement rate. If you're creating Facebook ads, you must use images that look attractive. One of the advantages of making use of Facebook advertising is that it allows you can try different variations of the ad , and then select the one that has the best percentage of engagement.

Concept: write a flawless piece of content for a digital marketing agency. The content should focus on the business niche of a digital marketing agency and list the Social Media Marketing Services you provide. Write the perfect content about your plan for business. It should include information about Marketing and sales strategies. Additionally, you should share interesting techniques for making it easier accessible.

Facebook Ads Goals

How do you ensure that your Facebook ads reach a significant amount of people?

You must use Facebook ads on your pages. If you're making ads through Facebook directly on the Facebook platform, it's difficult for you to reach an extensive number of users. So, if you'd like to find out what happens when you target your public is reached, you can create an ad on Facebook for your website.

Facebook Ads Structure

Making Facebook ads is not a difficult job. It is merely a matter of following the basic steps to create your first advertisement. To make an advertisement, you must follow the steps listed below:

Concept: Write flawless content on how to make sure that your online marketing company. The content should discuss five techniques that are viral and well-known in the field of digital marketing. Write a flawless article on Facebook advertising structure. It should cover the steps to follow when creating ads on Facebook.

Locations and Demographics

This is a great option for creating geo-targeted advertisements. If you wish to design ads for a particular place, then select the location from the options that are displayed after you click on this option.

Next step to select one of the demographic choices from the choices in the bottom box. You can choose an audience according to their age relationship status, gender, or gender.

Your Audience

When making an Facebook advertisement, you need to choose the people you want to reach. Facebook ads can reach out to the largest number of people. It is done by defining your intended audience according to different options under demographics like age, gender and relationship status as well as job.

How to make Facebook ads that have a great engagement rate. Before you can create an Facebook advertisement, you should know the different aspects involved in creating an attractive ad for your company. The most important thing that makes an advertisement effective will be its marketability to your target people.

If you're looking to create an Facebook advertisement that has an impressive engagement rate and you want to be aware the significance of the different elements involved in creating an advertisement that is attractive to the target people.

What are the elements involved in making an efficient Facebook ads are the following:

Text Description Text Description can be used to explain the you intend to achieve with your Facebook advertisements serve and how you can meet users' needs.

Tagline: Write a perfect piece of material on the online marketing company -- Social Media Marketing Business. It should discuss the ways you can reach your business goals with Facebook ads. Facebook advertising strategy. It should be between 25 and 35 words. This will assist in achieving a high engagement percentage on Facebook ads and entice customers to go to your website.

Text of the ad The text of the advertisement is where you write the text of your ad.

Categories and Subcategories The two choices are utilized to create relevant ads for your company. If you are planning to create an ad advertising a Facebook page, then select the category option to be Facebook pages and the subcategory as photography.

It is essential to select the right category and subcategory to run your ad as it will allow you to display relevant advertisements. If you don't select the right category and subcategory, Facebook will display your advertisement on pages that are not relevant to it. This can affect your business in a negative way. Therefore, it is recommended to be cautious when creating Facebook advertisements.

Images: If you are making your Facebook advertisement, the first thing that will catch the attention of your audience is an image of the advertisement. The image should be appealing and appealing enough to entice people to click. It should contain a few sentences about the purpose your ad is serving and how it will meet the user's needs. It should be white background to ensure that it is distinct from other photos of your page on Facebook.

Optional Targeting Details

It is the next thing to do: choose the appropriate subcategory for your company from the options which appear when you click on targeted targeting. You can also select the location and age group as well as gender for each of the adoptions. If you're planning to create an advertisement to promote your website's e-commerce, it's best to select an appropriate category and subcategory in the choices which appear when you click'categories as well as subcategories'.

~~Chapter~~ 11: The Reasons To Create An Digital

Marketing Agency?

Do you love social media? Do you spend the majority of your time using Instagram, Facebook and other platforms. This book was written for those looking to earn an income from part time work or an entrepreneur who can earn cash in a matter of days, if they're willing to do. (Some students have completed deals in just a few days). The results may differ.

Earn anywhere from 1000 to 10000 additional each month. In the United States controls most of the money. Who around you has your most? The business owners. best part about this industry is the fact that you're working in a B2B industry. Businesses owners earn the highest amounts of cash and may eventually collaborate with a customer if you require investment funds to expand your company. Of course, this is more sophisticated and may be years away for certain people. The business can be bootstrapped obviously. We won't even talk about the fundamentals of starting the business. These are common to all businesses. For example, forming the LLC structure, choosing a place to lease or lease, etc. We'll assume that you'll get that information online, and are only are interested in the Agency development aspects of the book. Be aware that this is a complete business , and that's one of the greatest advantages that most people don't realize. The majority of business owners do not want to be concerned over Social and you take care of their logins and their content.

CREATING A SUCCESSFUL AGENCY TAKES time and effort.

CLIENT Management

SCHEDULE the time to service your customers and

The process of building machines

Virtual assistants

Up work

Contracts

Administration

No more PARTIES in LA

Don'T FIND

126

W

E

WE ARE BUILDERING THE AGENCY LIKE A STARTUP

DESIGN TEAM

OPERATIONS

DEVELOPERS

Marketers

We want to have different types of PEOPLE employed by US.

Local Bars and Restaurants as well as

Family-owned businesses that are not owned by corporations.

Avoid importing Taco Bell into your CRM and then have your agents call

What is the Truth about Entreupanship

It's Sexy actually this course covers the variety of skills that you will require.

You're a call centre designer, legal team, and much more.

The aim is to build your team so that it can handle more jobs and better-quality clients.

Being an entrepreneur isn't only about Fast Jets, Pool parties and parties at LA, Lamborghinis. On YouTube there are annoying videos. It is important to learn and to work hard. Would you consider becoming an successful entrepreneur if it was simple? Some people would like to be boss, but they do not realize the work it requires.

I am in the Laboratory working on my brand new Lamborghini.

SMMA's Modern Rules of SMMA.

If a physician is satisfied , they will be able to recommend you to a doctor. After that, you can check Google and Yelp reviews. Be aware that value is the most important factor. If you can provide massive value, you'll understand the value you earn. Stop making Facebook rich and start making yourself rich. Some of the richest people of the present are those who use social media and related brands.

It is possible to turn it into a full-time or part-time business. The majority of people have only an income source. Everybody is searching for an income stream that is passive.

It's not for everyone.

Six Figure Agency

I have written this article in a style intended for people of all ages, however you need to have a passion for technology and business in order to succeed in this area.

Imagine your Agency as a startup.

Consider the ideal customer.

If you are able to offer a huge amount to those around you, you could be wealthy. Make use of your powers of observation whenever you visit Starbucks or the local café. You are the first employee, as well as a sales representative.

Basic Team (YOU) CEO/OWner etc.

Sales /

Design (Logo design, Social media Posts etc)

Marketing.

Every person who joins your team must understand your business goals and values.

You don't want to be a BROKEN BOY in 2020.

a passive person.

Yes, you can earn an income that is passive and will grow over time. the

Agency, however This book will appeal to those who are enthusiastic about Marketing, running an enterprise and participating at least in the initial stages.

SMMA is one most beneficial things you can do in 2020. There are those who will say they believe that market crowded. There will be competition, but you'll have your own Digital Marketing Agency.

Perhaps your aim is to quit your job and dedicate your time to your Agency.

The process of starting the agency will be simple, but you will succeed if are passionate about what you do. That's why I recommend finding that thing you love doing and not being more but could help with the particular company you're working with your own specific requirements.

There's always somebody consuming and someone else producing. It's not that the use of Social Media is bad but you can be rich and not just Evan Spiegel or Zuckerberg. Many of the famous brands and businesses are a little more adapted to what they are today. Like Starbucks it was already in place. Consider Starbucks today. The person who founded Starbucks discovered a new market and it has become a part of the culture into Society.

In this Business You are focused on Business owners. A lot of people think about a B2C business, however B2B is a lot easier to start making money from. The majority of businesses have an average of 10 percent of their budget, which could be put towards Marketing & Advertising. If you are involved in the field, you'll see how many owners receive calls from

(Fake)Google individuals, Credit Card Processing Companies and many more.

Yellow Pages and other companies to sign-up for their services that typically start at about 500 dollars per month. I'm looking forward to teaching you how to begin your business.

Beginning to get started with B2B is a breeze for the average person.

If you do not have anything,

* Find small-business proprietors to make payments of between 1,000 to 10,000 per month.

Very little startup risk

* Business start-up time is quick.

Learn from those who have already done it

* Study how to use the Agency Formula.

* How to locate Agency Clients.

* Each pitch will result in one client. (rough average

Create your own sales lead generation and sales Pipeline

* How many businesses have you met or driven to this morning?

Nearly everyone you are advertising might be a customer.

* Establishing the Right Mindset

Stop browsing through Social Media and get paid for it.

The process of setting up a website.

Utilizing Tools online, you can design a professional website with no prior knowledge.

Pages of the Website Site

Services

Contact

About

FAQ

Team

KDP income guarantee Build an income of six figures with SMMA's Secrets of SMMA.

Learn about lead generation and the fundamentals of marketing. Content Marketing Agency.

Content Marketing

Google AdWords /Analytics

Virtual sales Agent.

Outside sales agents.

You can also create your blog, social media pages, or a Facebook page.

Naturally, you can outsource everything but you must to know the areas of Digital marketing interest you. If you're the type of person who has no passion for Social Media & Marketing then why would you read this book?

It is possible to use free web builders such as Wordpress, Weebly, Squarespace and others. They will have a modest cost, however they are mostly drag and drop-based. So, coding isn't required.

Website Leads

Certain marketing strategies aren't designed to produce instant results.

Project Managers

Web Developers

Graphic Designers

In the range of $50-100 per year , you can expect to purchase a decent amount of me in or website builder . I strongly suggest using a content management system, which includes things like the shop on a phi square Wordpress, Weebly and many other platforms let you update and post content in your own.

For SEO rankings, I would suggest setting up an agency name with your city , or the particular niche you wish to target . You can use the name Dallas Texas marketing so-and-so or Dallas marketing, for example, in case the city you are in has big client base and you would like to grow in your local. This is what you need to do.

Selecting an Agency Name

If we hear a name at some point, we can become frustrated after purchasing business cards, registering the domain. Consider your name when you are on an interview and consider the various aspects of your name. What will it look like on a small Display or a larger display.

The name should be something that is able to stand out, but does not have to be make a brochure.

When you are building your client base you're advertising your company. Our approach is simple, but it is also strategic.

We assist people in attracting customers, while also increasing our rates as we go along.

If someone approached you, it was your local Sushi restaurant or Bar

Working with small Owners of businesses can be challenging certain types of owners may not be fit into your long-term strategy.

Beware of getting involved in Technology your primary goal is to communicate with people who run the business on an individual level. Do not spit out your information, even if you are knowledgeable amount about the subject.

Connect with the Business through the eyes of the owner, not only in relation to marketing. Naturally, you don't want to be a food merchant.

Web Developers

Abstract Names and Straight Forward

Abstract names for agencies are very common, and generic names are also acceptable. Each of them has advantages with Generic names that have a simple formula for replication and scaling across different cities.

I would suggest you create an Style manual to provide all the options you can accomplish within the Brand world. Create a style guide which employees could read about the brand, playlists of songs, colors, and everything else that is your Brand DNA.

SMMA is not a new concept.

Retainer rates for monthly retainers like $300,400 are ideal for those who are just starting your company, however as you expand you may never be in a position to accept one client with a budget of less than $1,000 because your rent and other costs are expensive. It's best to keep fewer clients paying more.

If you're unfamiliar with Seo it is possible to find the writer who writes about SEO to assist you in establishing the site, but it's better to know at a minimum the fundamentals to be able to do your own in SEO and building your brand's image. SEO is a term used to describe search engine optimization.

ux

What you'll need to ensure is that you include the specific area or niche you're targeting on your services and on your website , so for instance, let's say Dallas and you could compose something in the vein of the services you're seeking an agency for social media marketing in Dallas. We help small businesses in Dallas increase their online presence through selling and marketing on social media and you'll continue writing and traveling around your time in the city, and what you're looking to add your website.

If you're interested, to build your own website, you can make use of the Builder like Weebly and then purchase/build your own website by using a template builders. A majority of agencies will be satisfied using an Informational site builder similar to this. For 5-10 pages , that's probably the Max you can have.

Your Name Doesn't Have to be anything crazy. One thing to consider is Do I require a social media presence for my company? What can I do to approach owners and offer them services that I do not have a followers on. Based on your industry, it is simple to stay clear of. You must believe in the confidence of your company which can Trump your negative thinking. It isn't something you can be approached with confidence. You could make significant profits, however it is not for everyone.

You always pay for what you get So the more money you spend on your site on all things , the more professional you'll appear, but there's something to be stated about bootstrapping but not over-funding. That means you need to make use of human capital or even your own funds to grow your agency.

You're now a company owner, and you'll be speaking to other business owners. It's not too scary. It's possible to meet the most interesting people in doing this. Don't be a victim of the hateful. Many people won't be able to comprehend what you're doing. It may be your Rags to Riches tale. Particularly if the person is

You could also make money from your site in the future. The benefit of having your own domain is that it's different from Facebook, Instagram, Twitter or any other platform that you control it on a certain level. Facebook may alter their algorithm, among other things that could ruin your online presence. A well-designed website can provide hundreds of Instagram followers and likes on Facebook initially. Since it's simpler to create a quality website than to build a Facebook page that has thousands of Likes.

One aspect of the branding is the look and feel. The logo and colors matter, however the essence of a brand lies in its depth. Logos form part of a brand's identity, but they're only the beginning of the Ice the iceberg.

Branding is an essential part of your business, as well as for your clients and for yourself. Good branding isn't just about logos. It's about the entire process and the world.

Imagine your brand's image for the agency. For example, a rockstar. A heavy metal soundtrack won't work as a brand

The process of creating a successful brand is hard and a bad client could damage your image.

A lot of business owners are successful in running their businesses, but they don't know what's behind the Power of Social Media Marketing.

A well-established brand is the best method to attract new customers.

Sales CRMs as well as Lead Generation

There are websites like Yelp to discover prospective customers and leads. Hubspot, Bitrix24. One of the best features includes Bitrix24, Hubspot and the Hot N New Filter. This feature lets you to find restaurants that are recently opening in the city. It is common to hear the term CRM frequently within the Digital marketing World.

A CRM is simply an Advanced Contact Listing. The most popular ones are Salesforce, Zoho, Hubspot, Bitrix, Freshsales to just several. There are many more to be listed, but try some to determine what works for you. Utilizing the data from Yelp you can begin making notes and track the calls that you or your sales reps make.

The most important thing to know is to not be a victim of rejection. Because you may be cold-calling small business owners, there will be many who hang up on you.

In your CRM, you can keep pricing data as well as other details you may have discussed with your customers.

It is possible to make use of Excel as well. Simply copy and paste the information from Yelp into Excel or google sheets. Google Sheets is the free online version of Excel.

Learn to measure and track everything. Which sales call did you make today?

Virtual Call Center.

Commission Only

If you make a post your job ad on Indeed, Craigslist and other job boards that require commission only, you'll be unable to locate sales agents who can be working for you. The only method to locate Comission sole agents would be to conduct direct recruitment via LinkedIn as well as in person. I recommend that you have the base pay.

Base Pay

You may hear about Nurture in the field of Sales. It means that you will need to contact and follow-up with the client several times. Initial call: send an email, follow up call, etc.

There's a saying that says: Always Be Prospecting!

What we really mean by this is that there's always going to be many different ways to connect with clients. Your perspective as an agency owner will differ from that of the sales rep. What I'm referring to is, look at your business is it really the case that you be able to convince each and anyone you know about your business idea if you do it for an hourly wage? is a bad thing. If you're aiming to become an effective agency owner, you need to be able to delegate sales, however, you should also be excited about selling yourself since even when you're not in the trenches calling cold each day to try to convince clients to join the phone to sign contracts, you must be able to generate the same enthusiasm as a sales rep. also suggest taking a look at the book by Grant Cardone, 10x rule.

This will be extremely helpful when it comes to the subject of the cold calling method to this book. The book is encased with a tough exterior and is also the strategies that are among the most important ways in which will be used to acquire clients. There is a variety of methods of conducting marketing other than cold calling there are a lot of options to consider but the majority of the way this strategy is designed to be successful will be involving the development of an online call center or, if you prefer to have a physical place are you able to have one?

I have always said that the best solution is to have both. Some prefer to work in a place for work while other prefer working from home. let people observe how other people work. are aware that one person could be awful to others when they're at home in a quiet space. However, they could be totally comfortable with other people. This will help your agency's manager I'm likely to like to go in to see my employees working and other activities similar to that but everybody is different, so you must be flexible but also to be agile, which is why, even if you're working in an office setting, you must have a robust remote culture in which everyone is connected via the correct communications will produce greater results and also just pure leaf. are many businesses that don't care when you leave or clock out, they treat you as an employee.

I'm not really concerned, obviously my customers will not go to Mike's, I'm saying my sales reps will not be able to be able into a department, say to process credit cards and social media passwords for businesses or anything similar. I do my best to keep things clear. would like my sales reps to be aware of what marketing is. I would like my engineers in the coding software to understand what the sales reps are doing!

I'd like to have my programmers and Engineers to speak about programming with sales reps to explain the process, and the reasons why I ask my sales representatives call engineers to ensure that everyone understands what goes on in the business and it's important to be the right kind of business owner.

And I'd always advise you to follow the same procedure and that's to go in the trenches and don't be afraid to pick up the phone for a few times, even if you've gotten a bigger role in your business don't be scared to come up with cold emails to send out there are so many ways to do it and if you choose to take the attitude that I'm good at something , your business will not succeed which is why I like it if it were the physical location for a restaurant, you could do similar thing when you notice an extremely busy Q. You may have to work on your business but that's beyond the point since I believe you're well

146

aware of the concepts and the concepts in this book.

Voice search is growing in popularity, so keep that in mind when creating the content for your site. Consider how it would sound when someone conducted the search using a voice for my company.

Participate in networking events

In-person networking is still effective and is very effective.

Visit other membership organizations for businesses as well as attend events and talk to others. There are plenty of events where which allow you to meet small-business owners and give your company cards on to. There are also occasions through EventBrite and Meetup.com

If I refer to a 10-day series of networking events, I'm not referring to an events for marketing on social media because the majority of them will belong to the exact same business they are. I'm talking about topics that you are interested in and which will naturally open an exchange of ideas with participants after an example that I like. I'll share some of the things I attend which cross-reference with social media users and this isn't likely to be the same people who are perfectly cold calling for instance on Meetup I could check out classes for yoga or meditation or oral, and so I may attend the blockchain conference on various topics with different themes. I could

Provide value to your customers and you will always earn income.

Find all sorts of odd events both paid and free events that I'd like to go to because they appeal to me, and when you've got an in-depth mutual interest in the subject matter, naturally people will inquire about what your business and the type of company you're operating and the final decision is yours to decide if you'd like to play the salesman card or be able to ignore it and make it appear more important, which is its own merits and advantages. Away MTG when you don't rely on it too much. If you have a great website that you are confident your customers will be able online and be interested and investigate the website. You can then achieve that by having an air of mystery surrounding you can aid in knowing the right way to go about it If you're valuable in your own right, but if you're at an event where your worth isn't the greatest such as there's certain occasions where keynote speakers are featured and the like.

WEB DESIGN AGENCY

UX DESIGN

ANDRIOD

IOS APP DEPLOYMENT

Other Services

Cyber Security.

SMMA

Creative Side

Creation of content such as video and Photo. Making money from Facebook ads.

Your results from content creation will take some time to master. You'll create new formulations as well as templets.

Find the right niche.

Everybody has a niche they may already be interested in.

What's your vertical? In the beginning, I suggest beginning by choosing a vertical. Your customers could be lawyers, doctors Restaurant owners, and so on. Each type has its own cons and pros. Every company has the option of a marketing budget. It is possible to offer a no-cost evaluation or audit. If you are able to present them with facts and figures you'll stand over the rest. Tell them that they face an issue and provide an answer. There's about 40 million businesses you could present to.

Everyone has preferences and areas of interest that you could connect to your Agency. Check out your past and the companies you collaborated with.

There's no correct or wrong choice, however there are certain items that will benefit you more than things that work for me. I'm sure you've got something that you already know isn't related to the particular industry you're not in or an experience that you could focus on that will give you the first choice of packing a.

Locating partners and vendors.

There are also local web writers, graphic designers, copywriters who can help you with the work of your clients. You can utilize Square to deliver invoices to customers. In the end, you'll want to concentrate on big concepts and not on daily tasks. The first person you hire is a person who will help you manage passwords and manage all your logins. Because you will be handling the accounts for other people, trust is crucial. You may use Fiverr or other websites to create a social media post or any other type of product for your customer.

Always remember the more value you are able to give back , and the better reviews you get, the more customers you'll draw. Your profits should be about 30 percent. 1 customer for 1000 dollars a month. Imagine how you could improve your life even if you could have 300,500, 1000 or 2,000 more per month. It's easy to get caught up with a Ferrari and be billionaires, but consider just how little it would mean to the average American. This business model is a good one in the early stages of adoption. Once enough people start applying the ideas in this book into action, the market will become overcrowded.

It is important to know what you will get an Wordpress site designed for. It is important to know the requirements of the client and know how many pages are required. In the end, you need to be a full client of an agency.

Aiming at small business owners

Bread & Butter leads

Locating local business proprietors who you can "partner with"

Each person you be a customer for could be the subject of a case study.

Small-scale small

I suggest creating an Excel sheet that lists all of your partners and the price each costs for a website or for Google ads and so you can have a list of sites that you can base your decisions off of.

Establishing Agency relationships is also profitable as they can introduce you to customers. Based on how you approach - you will create the basis of a relationship

for instance, if they know that you are a specialist in marketing for dental and you needed assistance in the area of Logo Design for a small client. They may refer the dental patient to whom they are confident that you are able to deliver on your Promise.

Examples of Pitches

Calls from cold, Cold Emails, Instagram DMs, Social Media Posts, Youtube Videos. How can you attract clients? We will make use of cold calls, in-person visits or if you have to engage in digital cold outreach, then email only. Don't send out pitches to all businesses owners only on Social Media. Your paid advertising will be targeted at business owners, but only in the initial stages .You may also employ sales representatives and make your sales funnel and sales pitches. Be respectful to those around you. You could say, man this place is amazing, but it's not.

I'll assist you or give return your money. Don't be shy about offering an exchange or refund. Every business can offer charges or refunds. Retail stores suffer from reduced sales of the items sold. Things that are expensive online may offer higher refund rates obviously offering low rates is one of the goal.

A good system in place for all interactions can help us measure and assess our processes.

Being aware of technical aspects and external elements like broken hyperlinks, typography, etc. may be essential, however I'd rather have a cheerful and optimistic sales rep with no experience over someone who has but negative.

Managing risk

Start with Local and Small businesses to establish local and small

Once you've mastered the necessary skills and a plan now is the time to go out and begin searching for clients that are genuine for your company. Small business owners are easy to meet.

Search for companies within the industry or niche that you want to market to and be prepared to talk to the businesses you are interested in.

Cold Calling

Find important contacts and decision-makers via Yelp or Google. Add the contacts to a spreadsheet or a crm.

Create a Google Voice number to make calls from your.

Don't forget to keep the time your first call or first time. The first call and the business more of an inquiry into finding out if you are a good fit for their requirements and if your needs have in touch with the owner's name. Another thing to consider is when they could be at the shop time. Don't forget the moment you made the initial call. your first time to the shop will be more an exploration of determining if you are a good fit for their needs . If they might be your requirements being connected to the owner's name, the time they could be at the shop the near future.

To locate people using Yelp or Google Just enter lawyer + your Zip Code.

Or whatever you'd like to explore. Call a few to try to see what you can come up with. Certain people naturally tend to specific niches.

You could also attempt cold emails. The information will be changed and it will likely to be spoken in your own words .

It is possible to transform an email that is cold into a call-in pitch, and reverse.

Once you have an entire team together, you will find more sales reps to set appointments or account executives. Communicate in the language of the customer. The pizza shop's owner does not speak any marketing gizmo talk. However, they need to know that you're competent. You can utilize Business language to communicate with your colleagues. think 80/20 rule is the best way to go.

Think about the Brand.

If you develop a distinct product like Tesla Tesla you'll not require the same strategies for marketing that you would use for the 20th sandwich place in your town.

Consider the many local stores which are competing against each with each other. You're becoming an ally for your customer and must been enthusiastic about their products and services.

The pleasure of watching Gary Vee all day is entertaining, but you have to be dirty in order to witness rapid growth. The local mom and pop will not have the Superbad ads , but you can anticipate a steady of stream of customers to increase when they have Facebook ads are on.

You cannot directly ask for payment to manage Your Social Media Services?

The most frequently asked question on the phone: What are your rates?

The prices we offer vary according to the amount of competition within your area. For example, if I were to offer you a the minimum for a blanket, it would be 699 per month. (Or whatever you want to think about)

Our pricing is based on the requirements to make your business known to your ideal client.. That stated, we are a small company and we're willing to work within your budget to create campaigns that still produce results.

(Optional)

Perhaps you are a part of a contract, but not

We don't have lengthy contracts like other companies.

. We operate month-to-month, so If we're not delivering results, you don't need to pay us. Are you looking to learn more about?

The cost of a 30 second slot during the Super Bowl will not make sense for a pizza place in the local area .

Digital

Every call must first ensure that you're calling the correct person or owner. You can't

Marketing and PR, what's the different. ?

make a pitch to the person on the person on the.

The reason you'll need to engage with business owners is due to the message of their brand. This means you want them to communicate their story and brand.

Video Marketing is equally crucial. If you are able to document the most as you can about your

CALL BAD COLD

Chumps can make poor decisions... the rule of thumb follows this pattern:

Hi, my name is John Anderson from Generic Agency's office. Are you the business owner at Generic Agency?

What's the matter? We provide social media marketing solutions for small-sized companies. (click /hang up)

Or

I'd like to speak together with you and discuss ways our company can help your business.

Would you like to schedule a meeting this week to demonstrate how we can help your business?

Packages and Prices.

I would suggest having around three different options. A budget-friendly one starting around the 500-1000 dollars range. What are you able to offer these? Do you only provide just one-time web design? If you charge too little you will not make any money. What can you do to complete the task and look professional? You shouldn't take anyone's money and then not follow through with what you promise.

The moment to end your meeting will be apparent to you in your mind in a meeting with a client. You could have a closing timing that is not right or too early.

There is a way to get something as like this. There's a lot in the marketing industry that you can avail. There are some who cost $1,000 for their SEO (What is that?) or $299 for Google Adwords? How do you become an expert and conclude your deal. If you have one patient each month, how much of this for the doctor?

Affording clients with high net worth is the best option, such as Doctors Lawyers, doctors, Plastic Surgeons etc. However, every niche can be profitable If done properly. If you can get an agent five leads per week, what is that worth? If you are able to recognize the value of a potential customer , you'll be noticed and make more deals. Begin with Facebook marketing, and then provide the possibility of an Email List. Facebook is also linked to Instagram. Email Marketing is still very potent. Even even Email technically isn't considered to be a social medium, it's still extremely powerful. I'd prefer having 1,000 email addresses rather than 1,000 Facebook likes.

Conversion rates are more effective.

Chapter 12: What Does To Close High-Paying

Clients

How many of you have thoughts of "It isn't possible for me or I'm not sure if I am able to meet with clients who are high-paying.", "I am an introvert. I am shy or uneasy to speak to the wealthy clients to whom must be dealt with sales."; "Selling is not my forte. I'm not skilled enough with selling and am not able to sell to customers with high incomes." With these thoughts of negative and troubling you lose confidence and instantly downgrade yourself as if you are unable to do what you can actually do. Finding nothing that can be a motivator is only going to keep you being discouraged and hesitant to try things. "Do or don't it is not worth trying." is among the most well-known quotes of Star Wars. Star Wars series that each of you has heard. So the first step you must take to market yourself to the highest-paying clients is to improve your own belief system.

Belief System

If you are not confident in your self, it will not make you any progress. This is among the major reasons that keep many people from acquiring high-paying customers. Selling and marketing high-end services isn't something you can do a 360 degree shift in just a few days. But, it's possible to create a business that is satisfying and rewarding. Achieving more clients who pay high is a possibility since it's not an accident so it has to be planned for. If you commit to developing and implementing the design regularly then you're on your way! A majority of your clients will be very high-paying customers within one few years! Let's examine what belief means. Our belief system of the core has been formulated and developed over the course of our lives through the many events we've experienced, which we believe to be true or not. Do you know that the majority the beliefs we hold are formed by other people, such as television, parents and social standards? But the problem is that most of us do not think about which beliefs we will be able to believe. In reality, our opinions are often based on the wrong interpretations of events in the past.

For a visual example Let's look at this metaphor for belief. Imagine a belief as an tabletop. Without legs or legs, the tabletop can't ever stand on its own does it? But what happens if belief isn't a thing? When you decide to believe in somethingand you've got references to back up your belief. The references are the particular experiences that prove the idea. In this instance the legs are the evidence to back it up. They are the ones which make your table top solid and, consequently, will make you confident about your convictions.

In other words I'll provide an example to give you an concept of belief. If you believe you're not great in Mathematics and you believe it, then you likely to have plenty of evidence to support your belief. Perhaps you've answered incorrectly during class for a number of times, or you did not pass the two previous tests, or perhaps your mom said something along the lines of "I'm concerned that you've inherited my genes from the department of math, my dear." It could be a myriad of other reasons that you can use to prove your conviction. Therefore, using the information above there are plenty of experiences that support almost every conviction you adhere to.

Its Power Of Belief

Let's see how powerful the power of faith is. It's either your beliefs help you or harm you. It could empower you or lock you forever. This short tale will show you the consequences of your beliefs. Elephant keepers have a fascinating method to keep their animals from wandering off. They secure them to a peg made of wood by using rope. This isn't logical on the surface, as the rope is no chance of holding a mature elephant. However, ask any elephant caretaker and he'll laugh and provide the following explanation: "When a baby elephant is born, the herder attaches the rope to a peg using rope. The rope will be strong enough to support the elephant. The elephant's baby quickly realizes that escaping the rope is ineffective. He continues to learn in his mind, even as growing older and the rope becomes too fragile to support him."

One day the circus accidentally caught into flames and the elephant was killed. He was huge and could have easily pulled the pole out of the ground and walked off to safety, but there was a self-limiting belief within his mind telling that he was not in a position to succeed and he chose to not attempt. As with the elephants, we frequently form beliefs that may initially be beneficial, but they can hold us back throughout our lives, long after the original motivations have been discarded. It can be summarized by a quote from Anthony Robbins - "Beliefs have the power of creation and also destroy." In relation to the famous quote about belief in The Star Wars series which I previously mentioned The lessons to be learned can be based on the scene in which Master Yoda utilizes power of the force to raise an whole wrecked ship from the swamp, then lifts it up into the air and gently sets the ship on solid ground like feathers. Luke Skywalker says "I..."I do not believe that." And The Jedi Master replies "And that is the reason why you fail."

A Belief in can empower you

In addition, I'd like to bring it up in this article, regardless of whether we can succeed in achieving the goal we have set or plan, it's generally our doubt or skepticism that prevents our commitment to the task. This can turn into a self-fulfilling prophecy in the event that things do not be as successful as we believed they should. The beliefs we hold influence the way we conduct ourselves , and ultimately an impact on our performance. How do you change your self-limiting beliefs into an attitude that empowers you? If there's a small voice telling you that you're not capable or you're not capable to accomplish it, change the conversation around to: "If I could help someone achieve the desired result for themselves , faster, more easily and more effectively than they could achieve it themselves I have all the qualifications I'll require."

How to Position Yourself as A Professional

When making a purchase or financial decision, all clients want to work with an expert with a clear and genuine solution to their problem. No one wants to pay someone who could waste their money and time because insufficient knowledge and skills.

For a marketer to succeed you must be different from the rest to attract customers. You're one of millions of fish in the sea of possibilities. What makes you stand out from other marketing companies who are in business? What is it that you can do to get clients to prefer your product or service over others? You're now the authority. You create a name that is sought-after by everyone since you're the ultimate expert.

Find Your Expertise

Many people are prone to claim "but I'm not an expert."

Sometimes it's real. It's possible that you're not the greatest you can be.

It's usually simply the fear and lack of confidence that plays on the mind. It's interesting that even after years in a field , and achieving consistently good results, many people will remain hesitant to claim that they are experts.

Consider it. If you're not confident in your abilities What is the reason anyone spend a lot of money on your business?

Don't be hesitant about the things you excel in. Be bold and bold. Be bold and assertive. Talk about your experience to others, explain to clients the areas you excel in the field, how and why you become an expert at your field, and what they can expect when they choose you over other people.

Consider this: Would the client prefer to work with one who affirms, "Well, I guess I can help people to increase their traffic and stuff like that," or someone who declares, "I am an online traffic expert"?

Be confident and definite. Be yourself. Your customers will appreciate it since it gives them faith in them to collaborate with you.

Create An Expert Intro For Yourself

Find ways that will showcase your expertise to your customers. Interviews, videos, articles or even live chats   anything you could use to contact individuals and introduce yourself.

169

A professional introduction can aid in establishing your credibility. It's a powerful way to show your customers that you're the person you claim to be.

In your introduction in your introduction, you should mention your expertise area or your tagline or any catchy phrase you want to make use of to promote your company, your site, your product or service etc.

Be sure to choose one that is able to educate clients about your experience and expertise, what it can offer your customers, how you can help them and why they select you.

Do you have a Credibility Story to share?

It is crucial to share stories or previous experiences to further demonstrate your credentials as an professional.

So it is crucial to tell a story to increase your credibility.

It acts as a connection device between your audience and you. It aids in establishing credibility and trust, and then it inspires people to engage in action.

Step by step. Begin by sharing a your story of how you have struggled to achieve your goals to build attention as people are able to relate to you.

In the future, you will be able to describe your experiences and qualifications and the source of your expertise. This can be used to prove the reasons why you are more knowledgeable than others in the marketplace. Things like degrees, certificates and years of experience the first-hand experience of trial and error, etc. are all necessary to complete the task.

Finally, you are able to be able to share your personal experiences of achieving your goals, and also the tales of your most successful clients and customers. Tell them how they succeed by working with you.

Testimonials

The opinion of another person on you can be a effective instrument. A majority of people will believe in the words of a third party more than what the individual's words. We believe in the majority and find social proof more trustworthy and reliable.

If you're not receiving any volunteered reviews to assess your credibility, begin asking others to submit their testimonials. You can send an email your contacts to ask for their opinions about the experience they had having worked with your company.

If you're willing to go to an even greater extension, you may also offer coaching sessions for free for those who are would like to participate in an after-and-before experience case that will be published for a social proof endorsement on your blog or website.

Marketing Methodology

The way you market and present yourself to your customers will impact your image and credibility as well.

Many marketers still rely on the old selling method that focuses on themselves. For instance, "Look at how good I am. Pay the money, and then I'll be able to do it."

If you're constantly speaking about yourself and what you're doing well, whenever you interact with customers, you'll appear as an overbearing and fake professional who is aspiring to be. A good selling technique is to discuss ways to assist clients get the results they desire. For instance, "You need help? Here's what I can help you solve your issue. Let's take this. Also, this. What did it do for you? Then why don't you do it again? Please let me know if there's still a problem."

Customers are looking for a professional to solve their issues. The amount they're willing to pay will be directly proportional to the degree of trust that they feel in your abilities to achieve their goals.

In order to increase confidence in them, you must connect with them through the correct approach. Be able to show that you can assist them by offering positive and effective solutions for them. Provide the prospect with what they want and it will make them raise their hand and ask "Please assist me".

How to Identify and Qualify The Best Clients

To promote your service or product, it is essential to concentrate your sales and marketing efforts at a certain group of buyers who are likely to purchase from your.

Knowing your market can help you meet your customers' requirements. It is important to know who your customers are who they are, what they're looking for and what they can afford and more.

The targeted market makes sure that your business is targeted to the right customers and can help keep your business going in the longer term.

It is not necessary to be everywhere only be sure to work with the right people.

Identifying The Correct Segment Of The Market

A market is basically any group of current or potential buyers for a product.

So how do you figure the most suitable market segment to choose to target? It is important to determine which part of your market is likely to reap the greatest benefits by collaboration with you. Find out what your company offers to your customers. Find out your product's strengths and advantages.

For instance brakes that are anti-lock. They are standard on automobiles but the advantage to the customer is security.

While features are important and certainly add value to an item, the benefits can also motivate buyers to purchase. If you understand what factors will attract customers to purchase your product/service then you can determine the market you could be targeting.

In this instance that you could focus on a particular category of people who share similar characteristics, like parents with children. This is an illustration for market segmentation.

How to Determine The Qualifying Criteria

Once you have identified the possible segments within your target market the next important question is whether it is economically feasible and financially profitable to explore each segment that will meet your goals for business.

To help you make the right choice to make that decision, here's a list the criteria you should be aware of in making your decision.

Money

Are they financially qualified to use your services?

Needs

What are the issues (problemsor opportunities for improvement) the prospect has to face right now in their business? What is the most important thing for the prospective client to address these issues?

Desired Results

What are the goal of the client? What goals would they like to accomplish in a certain timeframe? What are their objectives? Are the expectations of the prospective client real? Are you able to assist them reach their goals within the timeframe that the prospects desired?

Expectations

What are the kind of "dream clients are you seeking? What is your expectations for your "dream" clients?

The commitment and determination

What type of commitment needed from the prospective client? Do they have a burning passion to reach their goals? Are they committed to following the advice of your coach?

Distraction

What could be the obstacles that the prospect is facing in their lives that could cause him to lose focus?

The Sales Process

Opening

The first step is to make sure that there are two aspects you should cover the first one is the reason of the meeting and the second is selling expectations and creating credibility.

What is the purpose of the call

When you are preparing to initiate calls with your client, it is important to define the reason of the call. A excellent way to start things off is to say:

"Hey here "client's names "I am calling you because you have submitted your application. I receive hundreds of applications every day, but not hundreds of applications that I've read. Your tale is the most captivating for me, which is why I'm offering you the opportunity to contact me. Are you still remembering submitting an application through my website? Is now a good time to speak to me?"

Setting Expectation & Establish Credibility

The next thing you need to focus upon once your client has accepted and is ready to discuss, you could begin by setting standards and establish trust for you to your client telling them:

"The reason we achieve such a high satisfaction rate with the clients that we collaborate with is due to the fact that we spend the time to understand them to be able to help them in a meaningful way. So , the way we work is that I'll ask you questions about your past and present experience and then I'll create a'success plan' for you. In the end we will be able to determine whether this will be an ideal fit for us. Does this sound reasonable?"

Understanding the needs of clients and Building trust by analyzing their situation

In the third step, there are three phases you should complete to better know your client and establish the trust of both you and your client. The first step is to have to understand their present circumstances. It is important to find out the things they enjoy, such as being asked questions.

* "Did you take the time to watch all of the videos? Not just those that are on our thank-you page?" * "What is it about the video that inspired you to apply? What was it that you liked most about the video?"

Additionally, you must know their history and present struggles by asking questions

* "I'm fascinated by your background, what's it like What's your story?" * "How many hours do you work currently?

* "Hong how long have you tried to make this work?

* "Are the people who are in your life, like your family and friends and your family, supportive of you?

goal?"

* "Why now? What's the main reason that's driving you to do this right now?

More than ever before?"

Find Their Dreams or Goals

"What is your ultimate goal? How much do you expect to earn each month for these next 90 days? And then, ultimately, what amount do you wish to be earning?"

"(Repeat your response to what they said))... After you've done the decision, how could it alter your life? What impact would it have on you?"

Also, you should discover the challenges they have to overcome by asking "Those are truly great objectives... Now is what's keeping you from reaching your objectives? What are your most significant obstacles as well as frustrations and obstacles?"

Conclusion

The effectiveness of your company's marketing strategy is contingent on the amount of customers you are targeting. You need to be able to see clearly in your mind about the audience you want to reach and know the most effective way to reach them prior to making your advertising. Making engaging ads that have a high CTR isn't a problem if you know who your ideal audience is.

It is crucial to know the location of your customers and the way they are informed about your business's services or products. You now know the importance of selecting the right category, subcategory, or targeted to a specific location. We also have details on how to write effective ads that encourage visitors to visit our sites, it's essential to be aware of how to create captivating ads that help us to grab the attention of users. The key to creating appealing advertisements is to know your target audience.

Where do people get information on products or services? In fact, search engines remain at the top in offering information, but there are other methods also. Certain people prefer to obtain information from magazines and newspapers and that's why printing media has always been relevant in our modern world. The majority of consumers today are turning to Facebook for answers to questions about items they're looking to purchase or services they want to take advantage of. This is why it's important to pick Facebook as a marketing channel for your business. You could even alter your current advertisements to one that is a Facebook advertisement to see the results it brings to you. If you're employing online ads, you don't have anything to worry about since there are effective methods to monitor the effectiveness of your ads. For Facebook advertising, you'll be able to track the number of people who clicked on your advertisement , and also know the amount of clicks that resulted in leads to your website. You could also alter the appearance of your ads and the landing page based on observed customer behavior data, in order to increase the number of clicks.